Property of
John Zannini

The Skier's World

by Morten Lund

T
SKI
WORL

Photographers:

Norm Clasen
Hanson Carroll
Bob Kreuger
Fred Lindholm
Fletcher Manley
Kim Massie
Peter Miller
Del Mulkey
Paul Ryan
Barry Stott
Bob & Ira Spring
Peter Wingle
and others.

HE

ER'S

LD

A Ridge Press Book/Random House, New York

Editor-in-Chief: Jerry Mason
Editor: Adolph Suehsdorf
Art Director: Albert Squillace
Associate Editor: Moira Duggan
Associate Editor: Barbara Hoffbeck
Art Associate: Mark Liebergall
Art Associate: David Namias
Art Production: Doris Mullane

Prepared and produced by The Ridge Press, Inc.
Library of Congress Cataloging in Publication Data
Lund, Morten.
    The skier's world.
    "A Ridge Press book."
    1. Skis and skiing.   I. Title.
GV854.L73   796.9'3   73-4727
ISBN 0-394-47963-7
Printed in Italy by Mondadori Editore, Verona.

To all those I've skied with

Contents

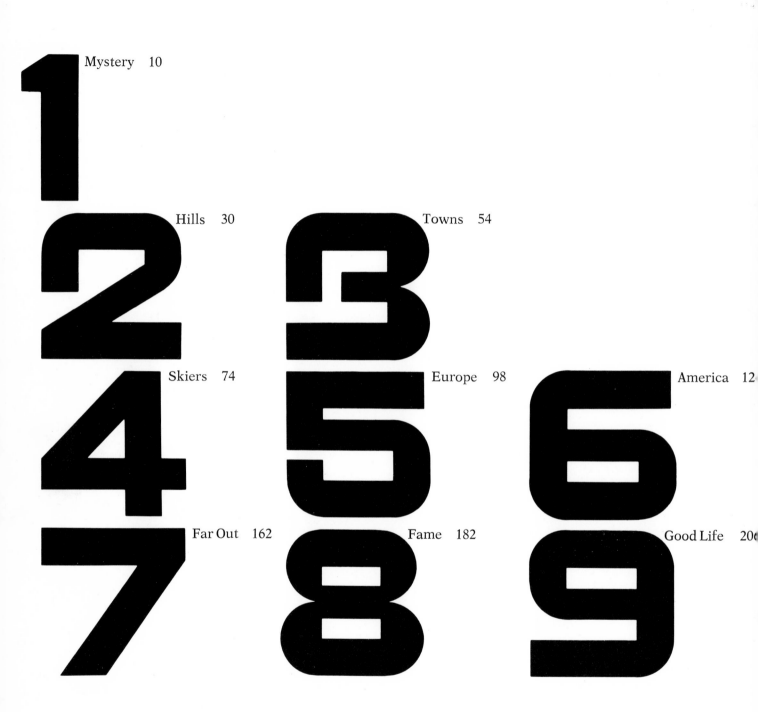

10

ACKNOWLEDGMENTS

The experiences underlying most of this book are owed to my work as an editor and feature writer for *Ski* Magazine. Its editor-in-chief, John Fry, has constantly pressed to make the magazine, and consequently my assignments, as wide-ranging and innovative as possible. In no small measure the authenticity of the writing herein is in debt to John Fry's zeal.

In addition, I am indebted to Fry for reports from several of his own itineraries, and to Mike Brady, *Ski's* correspondent in Scandinavia, for expertise in the historical background of the sport.

I gratefully acknowledge, too, the contribution of the fine ski photographers represented herein. Skiing is a visual sport above all, and most ski photographers are in the sport out of a real affinity for the values of skiing. In working with those who both shoot and ski well, I have had some of the most pleasant moments of all. I especially mention Peter Miller, Kim Massie, Del Mulkey, Paul Ryan, Fred Lindholm, and Barry Stott (at left), all of whom have a quality of enhancing any story simply by their presence.

Then there are those who have shared generously some of the journalistic travail—the rough travel and fast schedules—involved in bringing off a series of stories, especially my wife Bea, whose competence in handling complications and whose enjoyment of skiing have made it all humanly possible and worthwhile, even though she had to learn skiing the hardest way of all—from her husband. Others who have provided help and morale include my two brothers, Erik and Jon—ever since the days of bear-trap bindings; Alan Baker and Bill Hazen, who came through the Arlberg stem era with me and still have unflagging enthusiasm for new forays.

There is another debt to acknowledge—to those ski technicians who have worked, in part selflessly, to set my skiing and thinking on proper course: Bill Briggs of Snow King in Jackson Hole, Wyoming; Junior Bounous of Snowbird, Utah; Mikki Hutter of Salzburg, Austria; Clif Taylor, the originator of GLM; Karl Pfeiffer, of the first comprehensive GLM program, now at Bromley, Vermont; Jerry Muth of Vail, Colorado, who worked out the American version of the GLM wedge method; Willy Schaeffler, Bob Beattie, and Mickey Cochran, United States national team coaches.

The first chances I had to write about skiing were provided by Ezra Bowen of *Sports Illustrated*, who encouraged my interest. But before all others were my parents, who skied because they loved it, and who imbued me with that feeling—from the time I was three to the present.

—M.L.

Helga Lund, the author's mother, and the author, age five.

To be skiing is to be in a world not of man, but of light—an alternation of sun and shade, sparkling, evanescent, existing only in the moment.

To be skiing is to be in the sky's play of color on the snow, with azure going deep overhead, and magic shapes sailing and slipping high toward the sun, bright, billowing, and begetting, a shifting, unceasing, wondrous display.

To be skiing is to be in among peaks shimmering back to the horizon; other peaks lie beyond and other peaks beyond them. Always a beyond.

This is a skier's dream: a continent of mountains where the snow falls softly every day. Serrated escarpments frame a movement: skiers swiftly track down sculpted sides that shear like thundering cataracts far, far down. There is no sound in this world.

There is mystery here, the mystery of a different world, and the mystery of an inner world, too—of the body and its fabulous capacities for quickness and compound movement, a final gift of the gods. There is magic in instinctive responses to terrain flowing underfoot, and in the confidence to leave earth and to experience time expanding in indelible seconds of flight.

There is the mystery of partaking of an intimate, right, and destined relationship to a whole world of snow, rock, and sky—the skier as one with crystal, ice, and surging slope.

There are other mysteries.

There is the mystery of sport. The sport of animals preceded the sport of men; the playful survived and conquered; sport was preparation for survival. Now that sport no longer serves to sharpen survival skills, it serves to effect advantageous release of survival passions. Man today rides a current of unseen, impersonal, unpredictable changes and he himself is powerless. Yet continuing impotence is destructive to the psyche. In skiing man has an obvious, immediate challenge against which to exercise primitive power, to find

MYSTE

RY

The mystery of skiing
inheres in the color and play
of light in the skier's sky,
and in the infinitely
varied beauty of far places,
as in British Columbia's
Cariboo snowfields (above)
and Les Arcs (pages 10-11)
in the French Savoie.

Kicking up a trail of
powder: Tom LeRoy on the
loose in good snow
on a good hill (left).
Equally satisfactory:
A soaring jump, and swoop
down endless white
bowls under brilliant
skies, as at Sun Valley (r)
in spectacular Sawtooth
Mountains of Idaho, whose deep
powder is typical of that
lavished on western states.

release in hyperaction.

Skiers have thus found a way of releasing part of the human being so highly developed, so little expressed: the aggressive, adventurous, conquering self. This explains why people in large numbers will ski, in spite of the cost in time, money, and stress.

Skiing is no less challenging than high-wire walking. The skier has to control the tilt of his skis to within a part of an inch. The skier's precise footing at high forward speed equals the wire walker's precise footing at some distance from the ground. Challenges continually shifting in direction, subtlety, and kind call for total concentration. This demand of skiing makes it a superaware state of being, with everything forgotten but sensation.

With other skiers a good skier shares laughter, good humor under stress, the sense of adventure. He shares his pure, natural, uncivilized mastery. Every foot skied is a victory, every mountain conquered, an empire. First man into the deep nothingness of a white haze sets others following: down and down with him, sometimes fighting thick wayward snow, sometimes losing direction in white halos of light and blind in high-streaming snow.

There is mystery in the delight of the senses—the smell of the evergreen, sharp as a cutting edge, the touch of flakes, and the sting of driven snow. Wind records the plunge of the skier on every part of his body, an opposing torrent, now caressing and now ceasing as the skier stops.

There is the cold. The skier is warned by the sharp stab when he takes a deep breath. Nostrils close. Ears burn. Fingers grow leaden. The skier knows the cold.

There is warmth. The blood surges through the body as the skier warms to his own great, deep heat—a power from within, a volcano, an affirmation of power.

There is heightened awareness in skiing. In woods where aspen and spruce stand thick, the snow silts through the trees, and branches bear a gift of ermine. Skis

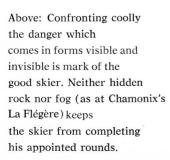

Above: Confronting coolly the danger which comes in forms visible and invisible is mark of the good skier. Neither hidden rock nor fog (as at Chamonix's La Flégère) keeps the skier from completing his appointed rounds.

Whether spilling
crystal (r), touring
silently (below), or
wedeling down Whiteface
Mountain in New York
(opposite), exuberance
characterizes the skier's
mood on the slopes
and pervades his après-ski.
Skiing allows one to
be primitive while
existing in a highly
sophisticated real world.

creak softly as they sink and glide through each glade. The only witness of the skier's presence is the skis' sibilance, cutting the crystal serenity of snow. The skier is aware of his world.

There's the mystery of pleasures, all equally sufficient—the pleasure of speed, the pulse of speed, the tremors of the skis vibrating in shock waves on resounding surfaces, the firecracker sound of cloth snapping in the air.

The absolute glee of the beginner when he finds he slides! It is no more stylish than a skidding on ice, and yet finally the weaving willfulness of the skis takes some direction—haltingly, comically, and successfully.

There is the mystery of forces, the straight line of the ski cleaving the curve of the turn, stabs of friction, the leverage, centripetal and centrifugal forces holding in and pulling out, inexorable gravity. The forces become the skiing itself.

There is the mystery of snow structure—that three atoms in one molecule carry the possibilities of glassy ice, of down feathers, of brilliant crystal. Snow falls as flakes locked with each other in a bushy bundle that settles slowly, draws in its ends, changes to a gem, and combines in clusters which spread and freeze in translucent sheets.

(Continued on page 29)

Varieties of light make
the skier's world.
Opposite: Mountain guide
carrying a pack glides past
glorious sun-shot cloud
and silhouetted pinnacles in new
snow at Jackson Hole,
Wyoming. Above: Backlit skier
comes over a ridge at Vail.

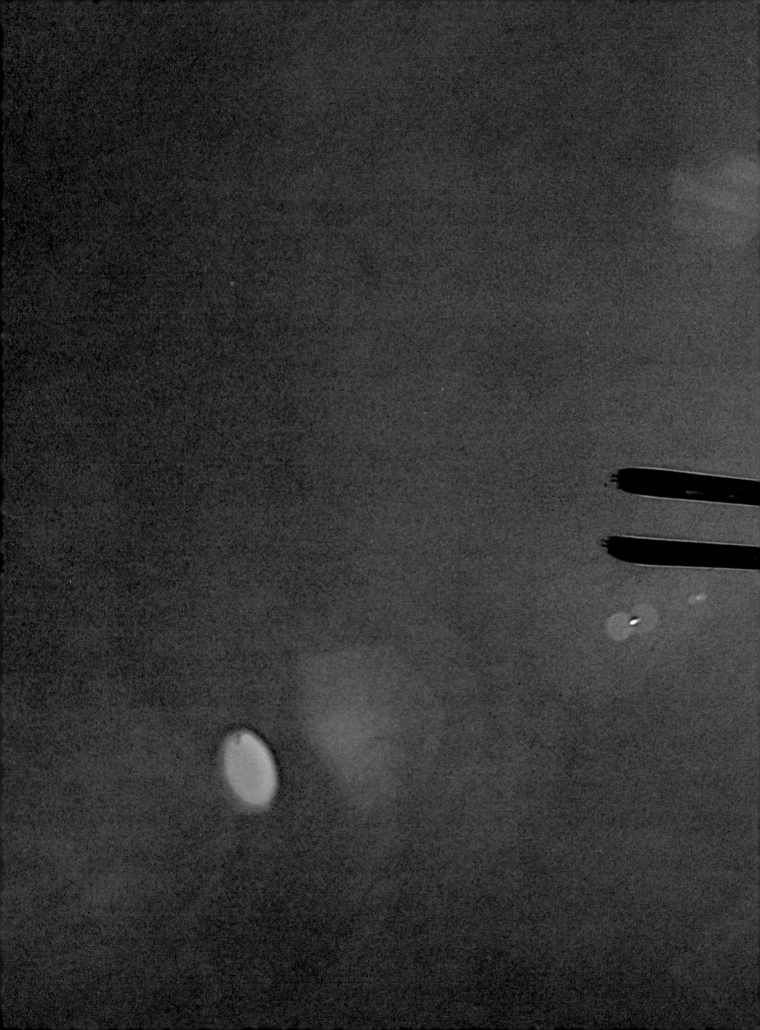

Preceding pages: Azure
sky aglow with sun's
light forms skier's
ceiling. Snow, pleated
and windblown, as
at Flaine (above), or
soft and sensuous,
as in Canadian Cariboo
(r), is his floor.

Ascending in France,
jumping in Scandinavia,
or swooping down Japanese
alps—these are the
skiing world's many joys. No
other sport is so widespread,
practiced in so many
forms, by so many age groups,
in so many places from
exotic to ordinary. The only
invariable constant is
snow—and even that can be
manufactured, if necessary.

Finally, the mystery that snow exists. Water was created as vapor inside molten rock. The primordial Earth, a holocaust, cooled to a hard surface. The vapor escaped from inside Earth, rose to a cooling sky, and filmy crystals of airborne ice formed. Fine cirrus clouds appeared and fell toward earth, the first snow.

The snow melted. Earth was not yet cold. But Earth cooled, and enormous devouring glaciers of hardened snow chased across entire continents, then retreated back to the heights to wait.

The snow ice is still in the high mountains. As winter comes on, it spreads lower, reaches toward the temperate plain, spreads to meet the skiers, spreads on all continents to lower terrain: Vermont, California, the Great Lakes, Appalachia, Honshu and Carpathia and Hawaii, Kashmir and Lebanon, Algeria and Australia and Peru and Chile. In each of these places, bodies cool and warm and experiment with ecstasy as men forget the joys of summer and return to the mystery known as skiing.

The original simple ways of skis have disappeared from the skier's world. The modern skier is adept at civilized dealing with machines and devices. Machines get him to the snow, steel lift devices take him over it. Sophisticated materials combine to produce skis and boots, marvels of engineering.

Ski cities become efficient, extremely pleasant machines for living, presaging a movement back from cities to the country, the first part of a selective dispersal that will lead to planned "new cities" that can change the face of nations.

This is the point in time on which the skier's world balances, the moment when the influx of complexity can slowly begin to diminish the perceptible rewards.

The skier's world cannot escape the world from which, in turn, it springs. Man will now refine, deepen, and expand his mystery or he will diminish it.

Ski domains may be as wild as Sand Glacier in Canada's Cariboos (opposite), or as tame as a group drag lift in Plander, Austria (above). The skier can choose to suit his present need: solitude or human contact.

2

Terrain connotes the Earth, *terra firma*. The notion of *ski* terrain includes the effect of going *down* it, and this makes skiing different from skating. Delight in a particular terrain, though, is not necessarily a concomitant of height, steepness, or majesty. Traveled skiers cite the Valluga, the Mer de Glace, and the Big Burn. Less peripatetic skiers are just as moved by the grandeur of the Lord's Prayer, a famous hundred-foot-high beginners' hill at Bromley, Vermont, or by that of one of the ubiquitous smooth mounds served by rope tows outside Detroit, Chicago, or Milwaukee.

All skiers are inevitably fascinated by terrain, yet without, by and large, having any idea why terrain exists in a bewilderment of forms, or why a particular terrain lies the way it does. A geologist, on the other hand, sees all mountains, peaks, mounds, escarpments, cordilleras—however solid-seeming—as plastic stuff, the pliable clay of a universal sculptor who continually, slowly subjects all terrain to conflict, defeat, dissolution, and rebirth.

It used to be held that there was no particular reason for the Alps to be so massively vaulting, or any particular reason for the Rockies to be so enormously extensive. The traditional scientific explanation was simply that all mountains were formed more or less by chance during the period when a young, hot Earth began to cool and consequently shrink a bit. The Earth, like a cooling baked apple forming its wrinkles, was supposed to have formed its mountains in random ridge patterns. But this "explanation" left much unexplained and new reasons for the creation of terrain were sought. "The scope and limitations of geology as it existed in the 1950's, before the present revolution, can be summed up as facts in search of theory. . . . There was mastery over 'what happened' but nothing but mystery about 'how it happened'" (Nigel Calder, *The Restless Earth*).

Much has been learned. The Alps were definitely formed by a specific "local" circumstance, not as part of a general global process. The same is true of the Rockies and all mountains. Science has deduced a step-by-step, on-going process that continues indefinitely, a process that builds and will build mountains.

The modern theory of mountain-building accounts not only for the most magnificent of ski terrains, but for lesser terrain and for the shape of the oceans, the creation of volcanos, the existence of deep sea trenches, and the likelihood of earthquakes at particular locations.

The theory is called "plate tectonics" —"plate building." It holds that the Earth's terrain is the result of a triple-layer arrangement, with the two upper layers moving about together over the lower. As the Earth cooled, a crust was created in the form of gigantic separate plates of basaltic rock sliding around over a softer mantle deeper down. On top of the plates rode smaller primitive "continents" of a light granitic rock, barely high enough to show above the oceans that covered the Earth.

The essential hypothesis of tectonics is that the underlying plates move about slowly in relation to each other. At their borders under the sea, they ram each other continually, a ceaseless butting duel of global dimensions that produces tremendous collision forces. The power to move the plates comes from hot rock pouring out of long slits called "mid-ocean ridges." The molten material from inside the Earth squeezes upward, cools, and becomes a new part of a plate.

Thus the plate is pushed outward by its own growth. The far edge must find somewhere to go. In the common case, as plates butt against each other, one plate "loses" and slides under its neighbor, so that it is bent down into the interior of the Earth again and remelted. This downward bending forms the ocean trenches.

As for the continents, they are still riding atop the plates and they too will collide eventually. When two continents strain against each other, one cannot readily dive under the other. The result is a tremendous head-on collision that causes each to buckle and heave skyward. Thus

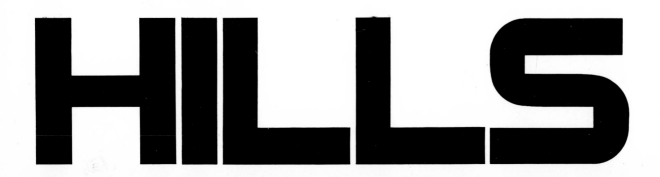

HILLS

mountains are born. Finally, the resistance of the continents to further compression equals the thrust of the underlying plates. Plate movement stops. The plate seeks a new direction for its movement.

All these movements are slow, typically at rates of two to three inches a year. But, over the 4.6-billion-year life span already allotted to Earth, there has been plenty of time for continents to collide, separate, and collide again.

Mountain-building is going on today as continental masses above and beneath the sea slowly, inexorably smash. The plates shift and dive and the continents strain and buckle. Earthquakes now are seen to occur frequently only near the junctures of plates. They are one result of plate movement.

The Alps, the world's greatest ski terrain, were formed when what is now Italy was a separate island riding northward on the "African plate." In the course of its progress, some eighty million years ago, it struck "the coastline of Switzerland." Then began a contest between the two granite masses. The ensuing heaving and buckling resulted in the continental edge of Italy overriding the Swiss continental edge and turning it under. The compression was enormous. If one could unscramble the Alps and lay the rocks at their original altitude, as they were at the start of this great collision, Europe would be sixty miles wider in a north-south direction than it is today. Sixty miles of rock continent were compressed and heaved skyward, inch by inch, quake by quake, to make the Alps.

The top section of the 15,000-foot Matterhorn was thus originally African, created from part of a huge African rock sheet, or nappe, which thrust its way for miles over the native Swiss rock. In Zermatt, at the base of the Matterhorn, your ski guide will tell you that the mountain is practically a Swiss national emblem.

The other great terrains of skiing—the Rockies, the Sierras, and the Appalachians—all originated in the same kind of continental collision that created the Alps. The resultant pile-up of rock has given us the proud "Big Rock" country that is the ultimate dream of the skier.

To ski well on small hills is no inconsiderable feat. But to earn respect in the world of skiing, you have to ski Big Rock sometime, somewhere.

Some people favor the Rockies, some the Alps, and others go to the Andes to find something less crowded. But beyond the choice of Big Rock ranges lies the choice of mode. There are easy ways to go into the high mountains and hard ways. An easy way is on an enclosed lift, wearing the latest gear, no more than an hour's downhill run from the glass-enclosed base hut, warmth, and food.

The other way is the way of the mountaineer skier, who is something of a throwback.

The mountaineer skier is a special breed who looks forward especially to those moments when he is in the remotest Big Rock—the ultimate and literal heights of skiing—alone. He wants no lifts, lines, or après-ski; at most, a few of his own kind. The mountaineer skier marches over the Alps' passes in the track of Hannibal's elephants, or over the top from Aspen and down to Crested Butte, or helicopters to the top of Timpanogos, outside Provo, Utah, and skis six miles down to Sundance. Common trails have no allure for the mountaineer skier; he abhors packed-out runs with what the ski pioneer, Sir Arnold Lunn, once called "the dead-tired surface of the *piste.*"

Sir Arnold not only founded modern ski racing, he helped found the sport of mountaineer skiing. He and his party would start at 1 A.M. and climb the rest of the night under "a moon shining with spendthrift silver" to top the pass at daybreak and then ski down in the early morning when the snow was at its best. It's still being done, exactly as Sir Arnold did it.

It's done most often and best on the

Opening pages: The Alps
of the Central Massif
as seen from above Mürren.
**This is the mightiest
terrain of all, an exaltation
of peaks in an extraordinary
part of the civilized
world, a place where Ullr,
the ski god, rules.**

Some hills skiers ski
are small and some
are very big. Among the
big are the high walls and
peaks shown here: terrain
over Telluride, Colorado
(1), pinnacles at Sestriere
(top) and canyons at
Courmayeur (above), both
in Italy, and towers
of Timpanogos, near Salt
Lake City, more
than 11,000 feet up.

classic tour of the mountaineer skier, the Haute Route along the backbone of the French, Swiss, and Italian border Alps. The classic trail begins near Verbier, Switzerland, or at Chamonix in France, and finishes at the Matterhorn above Zermatt or continues to Saas-Fee nearby. Either way is about sixty miles on the map but the natural zigzag of climbing doubles the mileage. Thus, the Haute Route is at least a hundred miles on skis, probably more—most of it above 8,000 feet. The first skiers to traverse the major part of the Haute Route—in 1903—were French from Chamonix, and the challenge, a sort of marathon of mountain skiing, has stood ever since. Only one party in five essaying a classic Haute Route trek gets to the end. The others are turned back by weather, fatigue, sickness, and accident.

The attraction of the Haute Route is not only in the challenge, but also in the breathtaking beauty of the exalted terrain, the comradeship of the expedition, and the experience of skiing as skiing once was: from valley to valley, across icefall and crevasse, across deep, driven snow, across hard crust, rough avalanche snow, and soft feathery powder that slowly sifts over the track.

Haute Route skiers bring coils of line for skiing roped up, if necessary, and for rappelling down chutes too steep to ski. Haute Route skiing requires crampons (shoe spikes) for icy slopes too slippery for anything else, and "skins"—fur-like strips the length of the ski—to tie on the bottom as a way to grip during steep ascents. Some guides carry altimeters, just as useful as compasses in reading contour maps.

Any two trips on the Haute Route are likely to be quite different. The Mont Blanc massif, over which the tour begins, is a prime breeder of wild variations in the snow and weather. It's not unusual to have to hole up in a snow cave or igloo along the route to survive a storm when the next cabin can't be reached on time. Cabins are maintained along the route, a day's hike apart. They have stockpiled food and fuel. Some have kitchens, innkeepers, and hot meals. None guarantees you a bed; there's no phone and consequently no advance reservations. But the floors, tables, and benches are always available for sleeping.

Two Haute Route parties are recorded in pictures on these pages. Members of the first included photographer Ira Spring and writer Harvey Edwards; in the second were writer John Skow and photographer Del Mulkey.

The Skow-Mulkey start was taken from Argentière, near Chamonix. Here, starting at 4,000 feet, they went up to 11,000 feet over the Chardonnet Pass, then down the Fenêtre de Saleinaz and down the Plateau de Trient over the Swiss border and down into the Val d'Entremont to Champex and Orsières, where, for the only time on the trip, the snow ran out. (The trip, for weather reasons, is almost always made late in the spring.) Skow is a good skier and was a relative newcomer to mountain skiing. He was amazed, no, stupefied, by the endurance required, the absolute need to keep slogging up that hill. The first climb to the Chardonnet took two hours, beginning at three in the morning. "The stupid goddam pass keeps receding!" wrote Skow, recalling how he panted in the wake of his guide. They skied to Champex in eight hours, having rappelled through Fenêtre de Chamois on the way. "By ten A.M." said Skow, "we were sitting by a small lake in a restaurant garden drinking Radlermass, a mixture of beer and lemonade favored by racing bicyclists and other desperate sorts. . . ."

The Spring-Edwards tour went from Argentière, too, over the Col du Tour. They went at a much slower pace than the other party because they had no guide. So they stopped twice at cabins before they came into Orsières on the third day. There had been an accident to some other skiers the previous day. An avalanche had killed four Swiss and badly injured two more.

Skow's group almost had an accident coming out of Orsières. One of the skiers slipped as he leaned over to fix his climbing skis and slid nearly 200 feet before he could get a ski pole dug in to stop himself. There is danger all

McLennan Glacier, British Columbia, a tumbled ice mass along a glacial run. Here the face of winter shows year in and year out—a rugged and persistent reminder of an age when ice and snow ruled the world.

along the route: a slip and a long, lone fall and, often, no return.

Both groups stayed at the Valsorey cabin, made of granite and about twenty feet square, one of the best-known shelters of the Haute Route. Upstairs is a dormitory with *lagers*, communal sleeping shelves with straw pallets; downstairs a wood stove, a sink, and a couple of tables. The hut, built to hold a maximum of thirty, had forty-five people squeezed inside when Skow's group was there. That was a pity, because everyone was locked into the cabin by a two-day storm, and then for three more days waited for the avalanche slopes to slide so they could be safely passed. Skow finally summoned a helicopter to take his people past the steep sides of the Combin de Meitin, where shelves of snow hung over the route like gigantic waves. Then they overnighted by making an igloo-type shelter of snow blocks; they had to wait for the helicopter to finish bringing in their gear. It took the party of twelve two hours to cut the blocks—square for walls, wedge-shaped for roof. They fitted the blocks into place with "delicate coordination of outside and inside crews." Then they all crawled inside and, shoulder to shoulder, went to sleep.

On the final leg down from Zermatt, past the "African" Matterhorn, Edwards' group had to rope up on the fog-shrouded Stockje glacier. Spring, as talented in mountaineering as in picture-taking, led the group along the faintly discernible edges of crevasses. (Roped skiing—at best—is difficult. Skiers must travel at nearly the same speed. In a fog, with the possibility of the leader going down a crevasse and the others having to brake and hold immediately, roped skiing takes a certain coolness.) Their way was blocked by an icefall. They backtracked. They tried another way. They were blocked by the ice again. Finally, with Spring nosing around the crevasses and past tall seracs—chunks of ice as big as buildings heaved to the surface—they eventually caught sight of tracks leading to Zermatt over the Z'mutt glacier. They were safe.

The Skow group endured a nine-and-a-half-hour forced march to get to Zermatt through a storm but managed to make it safely down (Skow wrote) to where "sweet spring water flows through a field of mountain flowers."

This is the way a most dedicated stratum of skiers celebrates a most challenging terrain. It's good to know there are still a number of skiers doing that seventy years after the Haute Route was pioneered.

The Haute Route is a minority experience. Terrain of a majority sort is met along Route 100 through Vermont. If Route 100 can be called "la Basse Route," the Low Route, nevertheless it's where more American skiers have begun their skiing than any other piece of road in the U.S.

The terrain of Route 100 is the busiest, swingingest, most lift-bestrewn in skidom. It runs 160 miles from Dutch Hill in Massachusetts, across the border of Vermont near Mt. Snow, to Stowe, the capital of eastern skiing, and continues northward until it grazes Jay Peak near the Canadian border—"the road that skiing built."

Ten or fifteen years ago, Route 100 was a pretty happy route. It was crowded on Friday and Sunday nights, but the Vermonters all got out in those days to stand at the roadside and cheer. "Keep Vermont Green" meant with dollar bills. The Vermonters were glad to see skiers.

Route 100 was the alley where you and your family progressed north with progressing skill. The goal was to one day skim together down the Seven Sisters, those fearsome turns of Stowe's fabled Nose Dive.

Bromley was the first Route 100 place to offer lift skiing. The barn-red base buildings have been a skier's landmark since the 1930's, when young Fred Pabst gathered together some rope tows he'd set up around New England and concentrated them at Bromley. Then he built two of his famous J-bars, the first good drag lifts in Vermont. Besides Bromley, in those pre-World War II years, there were only Stowe and Mad River and Pico in the state of Vermont with anything better than two ropes to offer.

Pages 38-39: Spires
of Canada's Bugaboos thrust
toward sky, an impressive
result of enormous forces that
formed earth's heights.
Above: In Brule Pass on the
Haute Route a skier can
savor the sense of adventuring
on the roof of the world.

On the Italian side of
Col de l'Evegue, with Mont
Tête Blanche in background,
a skier makes his way
along the Haute Route, questing
ground of world's most
serious skiers. En route:
Traverse between
Col de Chardonnet and Col de
Fenêtre de Saleinaz (l),
passing an alpine farm near
Zermatt (below), and rappel at
Col des Ecandies (bottom).

Then came the postwar boom.

Vacation-home owners who wanted one foot out of the city boosted Vermont's population. Permanent residents increased from 200,000 (only slightly more than the number of cows) to double that figure, and the transient ski population quadrupled. Lifts went up at Glen Ellen, Sugarbush, Stratton, Killington, Magic, Mt. Snow, Jay Peak, and fifteen other resorts as big as Bromley had once been.

The first high-capacity resort was Mt. Snow, "Walter's Wonder." Walt Schoenknecht led the way to the boom. He had looked over a desolate farm at Mt. Pisgah, near Wilmington-Dover, and had seen in it a wonderful place for lots of people to ski. Mt. Pisgah was a benign mountain; Schoenknecht knew better than anyone that a terrain did not need to be steep to be popular. Mt. Pisgah became Mt. Snow.

Walter saw that the reason for the low rate of return at places like Stowe and Mad River was that you couldn't get enough *people* on those mountains. Mt. Snow underwent a shaving operation. Long, wide ribbons of Vermont grass appeared on Mt. Snow, with trees left only as dividers. Lifts went in by pairs and trios. When the snow fell, Walter had a production-line operation; no trail there required much ability beyond the middling. No longer was the beginner-intermediate loathed, shunted to side trails and given the back of the mountain. And there are ever so many more beginners and intermediates than there are good skiers.

From the air on a weekend Mt. Snow looked like an ant hill. Every weekend, every month, new attendance records were set. Stowe and Mad River used to boast of a day when a thousand skiers were tallied. Mt. Snow began to report four, five, six and seven thousand skiers. On one day, Mt. Snow set the record which probably still stands. If it's been surpassed nobody wants to talk about it: ten thousand skiers on the hill.

Killington was the second "supermarket" to go in, built by Preston Smith, a tough-minded kid of twenty-seven, and a handful of twenty-year-old partners. With Smith driving an old bulldozer, they hacked their way in and put up a Poma lift. They turned the bowl at the head of Killington Valley into a place that could outdo Mt. Snow by giving more varied and widespread terrain to as many skiers. And Smith besieged the state for help.

The state of Vermont had always liked ski developers but not enough to hand them anything. However, Smith sat on the doorstep of the legislature until he had convinced closefisted lawmakers there was gold in his hill. He convinced them that they were foolish not to help him get it out. The legislature finally agreed to build a six-mile blacktop into the Killington base area.

Killington Basin was now ringed with lifts and packed with skiers at four base lodges. The beginner slope alone had three double-chair lifts going up its nearly level slope; Killington's two-mile gondola lift was the largest and most ambitious lift development in the East. Killington was the first to gross more than $6 million annually.

Killington's mountains were ringed with miles and miles of Killington-owned land. Pres Smith marketed this land to skiers who wanted a permanent, rentable home in Vermont. The trail under the two-mile gondola was laced with lots. "Ski right into the trail from your door." Oh, how the money rolled in!

Schoenknecht responded with a huge base lodge at Mt. Snow, while an original one expanded and grew to a four-story giant with a pool under it. An inn sprang up on an artificial lake—connected by a special, rocket-form lift to Mt. Snow's base. Walt's last public scheme called for a completely closed-in-glass "ski city" at Mt. Snow. It would have interior temperature control, palm fronds, boutiques, and air filtered of all its noxious fumes.

However, the Vermont natives finally got restless. Ian McHarg, the top name in ecological land planning, made a study of the Dover-Wilmington area and

Skier on Haute Route pauses
beside a serac, a block
of ice the size of a house,
cast up by glacial
movement. Besides regular
gear, *routiers* carry
ropes, ice axes, crampons,
altimeters, and skins
to keep skis from slipping.

Blizzard (above) engulfs
Valsorey Hut on Haute Route.
Skier (r) threads Col
de Fenêtre, headed for
Matterhorn (opposite),
which marks end of
the journey for many.
Route is open only in spring,
when avalanche danger
and bad weather are at a
minimum. Nevertheless,
weather cuts short more
than half Haute Route trips.

found that in ten years' time the then sub-divided land around Mt. Snow in the Dover-Wilmington area could have a population of 30,000 home-owning residents. This would make Dover-Wilmington the second largest city in the state. Stating the reaction of many Vermonters, John Christie, then the manager of Mt. Snow, said, "This type of development just sacrifices too much of the Vermont life style that must be preserved."

The Vermont legislature turned around in its philosophy and passed a couple of extremely tough laws limiting future development. Act 250 and Act 252 set "limits on the uses of all land in Vermont," wrote Dinah Witchel in *The New York Times*, "not merely state-owned land. They include guidelines for preservation of air, water and soil quality and a mandate that, among other things, future development on public or private land will 'not have an undue adverse effect on esthetics.'" Or, as one Vermonter put it, "You can't spit in a Vermont stream." Acts 250 and 252 not only slowed down or stopped most large-scale housing developments but made it extremely unlikely that Vermont would get any new ski resorts. The freewheeling days—when a Pres Smith could go in with a rusty bulldozer plus one Poma lift, and in ten years parlay *that* into the biggest recreation complex in the eastern United States—are over on Route 100.

Route 100 is a fine factory for making skiers but it does not figure largely in disputations among skiers as to which is the best terrain in the world. The partisans of the Alps go into rhapsodies over the Arlberg Pass, the Davos-Parsenn, Mürren-Wengen, and Val d'Isère-Tignes. The globe-trotters talk about the 6,000-foot descent from the Kitzsteinhorn and the five-mile run down the Corvatsch across the Engadine Valley from St. Moritz, and about the longest possible vertical of them all, off Mt. McKinley in Alaska, where it is possible (as the Swiss descent-specialist Sylvain Saudan has shown) to go 12,000 feet down into the valley, provided you have the time, money, and persistence to mount and carry through the five- to ten-day expedition needed to get on top.

Those who champion the American terrain in the West speak of the multiple possibilities provided by the squadrons of lifts at Squaw Valley, the double terrain of the marvelous snowfall at Snowbird-Alta in Utah, the double-exposure at Sun Valley, the sweep of Jackson Hole, the unabashed steeps of Taos in New Mexico, and the hidden mazes and crannies of terrain known only to those who live in Aspen year around and have worked out the secrets of Ajax.

Every good terrain has its bad moments. There are times when Aspen is iced up while Mt. Snow back in Vermont has powder. And there are times when the wind howls across the fabled Sun Valley runs with a ferocity that puts Mt. Washington—the windiest terrain in the world—to shame. On the same day the snow is sifting down to create good skiing on the top of Squaw, Alta and Snowbird can be full of mashed-potato snow. To speak of terrain in the abstract is a little precious.

However, to give the impossible a small try and attempt to define "the best": The length of the run by itself cannot determine quality. Nor can the vertical alone, or length combined with steepness. It is the *playfulness* of terrain that creates the best in skiing. A terrain of rises, drops, smooth gullies, mounds, banked sides, and roller-coaster curves gives the greatest texture of enchantment. The fun of skiing a massive snowfield depends entirely on the quality of the snow; but playful terrain is perpetually a joy. The legend of Aspen depends on this. None of the runs is spectacularly long, but there is such a possibility of variety, of zooming out and up, of snaking from one trail to another; if there has to be a choice, this quality of play should be uppermost in the judging.

There is a small mountain in New York, Song Mountain, designed by the late Austrian Otto Schneibs. It is not a particularly distinguished vertical or even a naturally superior terrain, but the genius of Schneibs has made each trail a lilting, spirit-fortifying run, no matter what direction you take down. There is more than magnitude to terrain. There is art.

That, finally, leaves us a last consideration about terrain: the fun and difficulty of handling it.

Terrain is rough, smooth, mogully, steep, flat, rolling, bumpy, easy, tough, and superb, depending on where it is and who's talking. Terrain, thus, is what your skis actually react to. Skis react to terrain strongly. It's not uncommon for skiers to come to a doctor complaining of a sore shinbone when what they have is a "hairline fracture" of the fibula, the small bone on the outside of the leg between knee and ankle. The break is not serious, but it hurts. Three weeks off skis in an Ace bandage is the usual prescription. The cause is the shock of terrain. A simple drop-off or clattering turn on an icy face can do it.

A fibula hairline is the commonest example of "terrain fracture," an accident in which the skier breaks a bone while standing up. The most dangerous terrain fracture is the spinal compression, the "racer's break." Happily, spinal fissures can often heal without a cast. The writer's wife, Bea, dropped five feet off a headwall on Copper Mountain in Colorado and got such a fracture. It took only three days strict bedrest and some weeks of careful walking to complete the healing.

No one has said skiing is a sport without risk, and yet the alert skier who has learned how to soften the impact of terrain will be taking less risk.

Bumps surrounded by little gullies make what is called "mogully" terrain. The skier who has learned simple turns soon comes up against this most prevalent of all terrain problems. Moguls are the mounds made by the skiers themselves. At the onset of the modern "short swing" or "wedel" turn, skiers began to descend any steep hill in a series of short turns. (The major function of a ski turn is not, of course, to change direction, but to brake the skier's speed.) Skiers mostly prefer a stable track and avoid the loose snow.

There are hills and hills.
In contrast to remote heights
of the Haute Route are
the hills of a much lower road,
Vermont's Route 100. This
is heart of northeastern American
ski country—the place in the
western world of greatest mass
downhill skiing below 3,000 feet.

Hills of Route 100 are playground of skiers from New York, New Jersey, and Philadelphia, but not of many Vermonters. Typical Route 100 scenes are cars at Little Spruce, girls at Mt. Snow pool, crowds at Glen Ellen base lodge. Good skiers at its summit (r) get a somewhat Disneyesque view of Mt. Snow complex below.

Antithesis of Route 100:
A trackless wilderness
in Canadian Cariboos filled
with unsullied powder.
Here turns are made
for sheer joy—not as
a split-second maneuver to
avoid collision with
one of an army of skiers.

Thus, skiers ski in each other's tracks and the piles of loose snow they create on turning grow higher while the tracks get deeper. After a storm, within a couple of hours of the trail being opened, the characteristic oval-shaped moguls appear on any section over twenty-two degrees in steepness.

Techniques for handling moguls have grown to meet the problem. A good skier can breeze through moguls like a lumberjack sprinting across a river full of logs. The basic technique divides into two approaches. The first is to go over the mogul, in which the skier "sucks up" his skis by retracting his legs swiftly as he starts to ascend the mogul, and then thrusts the skis down again hard as the mogul drops away beneath. This keeps the skis in contact with the snow, so that the skier stays in control. (If the skier takes the bump stiff-legged and gets thrown off the down side onto the next mogul, he is headed for disaster, or at least loss of control.) In the proper attack, the skier's center of gravity is displaced up or down as little as possible. The head of the skier rises and falls less than the rise and fall of the terrain.

The second approach is to "river run" the moguls, which means to turn so adroitly as to stay in the troughs or gullies. This takes a fine coordination. A good mogul skier combining "over the top" with the "through the trough" skiing as he runs a field of moguls at twenty miles an hour is an impressive sight.

Many skiers are troubled by the flat runout. Techniques for handling a flat have been advanced through racing techniques. Many, many downhill races have been won on the flat. There is where the *glisseur*, the racer who does well on the flats, has his chance. A good *glisseur* anticipates the flat, so that he comes to it with maximum speed. Then the thing is to make that speed last all the way across. The skier has to have good "edge control," keeping the skis flat on the snow all the way across, rather than turning them slightly up on edge (as in a turn). The skier who can keep a flat, "quiet" pair of skis all the way across will leave his less accomplished friends far behind. They blame their skis and think that the *glisseur* has "fast skis." The *glisseur* knows better.

He has another trick: putting his weight back to reduce the retarding impact of unevenness in the terrain. This is a simple shift to a sitting-back position. (The full sit-back of a strong skier with the seat of his pants barely off the ski is only a stunt.)

Air resistance is another major slow-down force that must be countered. To keep it to a minimum a skier goes into a "tuck" position simultaneously reducing air resistance (by lowering the body profile) and putting the weight back on the afterbody of the ski.

The dip or gully, the third most frequent terrain problem, calls for a technique exactly the reverse of mogul technique: The skier thrusts the skis down as the terrain drops at the near edge of the dip, and pulls the skis up as the dip rises at the far lip. This lets him go across a dip with good control.

The quiet, fast skier who moves out so smoothly ahead of his friends on a downhill run, who never seems to be fighting to get his balance—this is a skier who knows a lot about ski terrain. The relation of the technique to the contour of the snowpacked earth spells the difference between a man skiing aesthetically and a man who is just bulling down the hill.

Appreciation of terrain derives from an understanding of the origin and geology of the terrain, from having challenged terrain at its most remote and uncivilized (as along the Haute Route), from skiing countless variations man has put into terrain for skiers' enjoyment (as in the resort complexes along Route 100), and from study and refinement of technique through meeting problems in foot-by-foot descents of a hill. If he learns enough and skis enough, the skier can cope joyously with any ski terrain the skier's world has to offer.

The superior style and substance of a great ski town can make the difference between a ski trip and a *great* ski trip. A great ski town doesn't have to be big. St. Christoph, in the Arlberg Pass in Austria, has only six hotels, but its concentration on skiing as an art form is so intense that the air is charged with it, and a stay in Christoph becomes imbued with an almost palpable *feeling*.

Or it can be the après-ski places in a town that make it great. Two or three good après-ski places can color an entire ski week *en rose*. Down the pass from St. Christoph in St. Anton are the Post and the Krazy Kangaruh, respectively an après-ski bar and an après-ski night club, both absolutely alive every evening. When people say "St. Anton," they mean the Post and the Krazy Kangaruh.

If it's not après-ski, then it's people: an instructor who really brings you along or a scintillating spirit who creates an occasion out of an ordinary ski day. Or it may be that the whole town is full of amiable, handsome skiers and there's a special group that includes you. Great things happen in great ski towns.

Beyond all this, the great ski towns of Europe and America have a clearly definable style and substance. What is European couldn't possibly be American. *Vive la différence!* It is why you go over there.

The differences stem from differences in age. The European ski town traditionally overlays a very old, established mountain village. Zermatt and Sass Fee, in Switzerland, have records dating back to the empire of the Caesars. The people of Andermatt plundered Romans and Huns, indiscriminately.

European mountain villages, founded by a family or two with a streak of stubbornness and independence, were the result of a pioneering spirit not unlike that of the early American settlers. Instead of *across*, Europeans who were fed up, went *up*. Mountain villages got started as a way of reducing population pressures in the valley. Mountain men were hardier, content to subsist on less, to endure more. In sum, here was a population of skiers waiting for the sport to be invented.

The advent of the climbers—mad Englishmen who would pay money to go to the top of the mountains—made the village boys first into climbing guides. Then the enthusiasm for sport spilled into winter and the mountain boys became ski-instructor winter guides. Kitzbühel and others enticed Norwegians to come down with skis to teach their local people. Davos and Zermatt learned from the English who had learned from Norwegians. Alpine skiing, in the hands of tough peasants familiar with every precipice, became a distinctly more fearsome sport than that which Norwegians had exported. The central European mountain boys became—still are—the best downhill skiers in the world.

In the European ski villages, noted one ski writer, Mark Heller, "farmyard smells have been banished by suntan oil." Yet the older European ski town still has its peasant solidity. The typical town rises—hotel on hotel, pension on pension, châlet after châlet—by streets and stages up toward the hills in walls of dun, ochre, off-white, and pale gray, a muted vertical checkerboard of masonry, abutments, archways, cobbled streets, carved balconies, and worked shutters. The Europeans cut their trees in the past. They build now with brick, mortar, stone. This is style and substance, grace and permanence.

A European ski town is a natural feature, then. The wild incongruities of the American ski town have been avoided. Everything blends. Nothing sticks out, glares, or winks; Americans coming to town have trouble seeing the word *coiffeur* linked to the scroll above the door, or *Konditorei* lettered on the wall above the windows in modest pale blue.

This naturalness and solidity *par excellence* describe the queen of European ski towns, St. Moritz. She is the largest, the richest, most impressive, most

TOWNS

storied and complex Swiss ski town of them all, an example most rewarding to study. St. Moritz, basically, is a resort of quality. It has its own, and they are Europeans who matter, not because of money but because of family. St. Moritz is old Europe. To illustrate: A fashion editor once went to St. Moritz accompanied by a minor count who was also a photographer. In Paris, the count was simply another photographer scrambling around to make contacts and bring the right people in for the shooting. In St. Moritz the count was home. Most of the time, he ignored the fashion editor. "He could get a waiter at the Palace running across the whole floor by simply turning his head," she reported. "The deference everywhere we went was deafening. We got up on the hill one day for a shooting and he went into the Corviglia Club for lunch. It was not for the common people. I, the count's employer, was not allowed to go into the Corviglia Club for lunch."

St. Moritz also has the feeling of a spa, of a place where people come to *be*, not to conquer the hill. Well-to-do alpenstock-holding couples hike up the roads as they did on their honeymoon ten years ago and that, in spite of the *arriviste* notion of skiing as something here to stay, is what they are going to continue to do.

St. Moritz offers real alternatives to skiing. It has built a wide variety of sports facilities and built them to last. The town still has everything it erected for its two Olympics and it could start an Olympics tomorrow, if you will just work up a schedule. There's a Cresta run, a bobsled run, ski jumps, skating rinks, a speed-skating lake, a hockey rink, even a winter horse-racing track. For the tourist, there are a gambling casino, horse sleighs for parties, luges for the little kids who don't want to ski, special instructors who babysit for those who do, inns for the rich, inns for the not-so-rich, hotels for swingers (the Club Méditerranée has residences here), hotels for *grandes dames*, and even a few places where you can get by for next to nothing if you don't mind dormitory sleeping.

Most European of all: There is no such thing as that honorable American profession, the amateur innkeeper. Ah, no. The innkeepers are competent hotel-school graduates, or at least know the standards. And the ski instructors are trained by the state and have the same status as the local school teachers, professionally. What ensues, therefore, is a perfect understanding that the relationship with the winter guests is solidly founded on money, no bogus heartiness. It would be unspeakably bad taste for a Swiss to perform a service without expecting and extracting payment in proportion. You can let this take the edge off your stay or not.

The great hotels—the Palace, the Kulm, the Carlton, the Suvretta, and the Chantarella—stand around the town, looking impervious, bastions of the international set, a group that gravitates here to see themselves recognized, all moving with the same stately tread through the mirrored, lamp-festooned halls.

The Palace: This is the Badrutt Palace, the hotel where, a hundred and some years ago, Johannes Badrutt entertained St. Moritz's first winter visitors after cunningly betting some of his London summer clientele that St. Moritz was hospitably temperate in winter. He won—and Swiss winter tourism was invented at a stroke.

The Palace does have a certain reputation to uphold. The service is impeccable. I recall a dinner for three, with a waiter for each of us, and marvelous food, all for $10 a head; wearing a dark suit was *de rigueur*. Where else could you dine in a candlelit alcove so reasonably, and then go off downstairs to the King's Club for a very mild version of the rock world (St. Moritz does acknowledge outside worlds), including a live band and a couple of bar girls with electric blue hair?

To exceed St. Moritz as a spa, you would have to go to Bavaria, to Garmisch-Partenkirchen, Germany's largest ski town, which is a spa almost to wretched excess. "Garmisch" lies a stone's throw from Munich, and thus runs a robust route as the watering place of the city's elite, as

Opening pages: Newest
ski-town concept is La Plagne,
a high-rise, no-auto
village in French Alps south of
Geneva. Classic ski towns lie
in low valleys, second generation
in high valleys, and
third generation are up the
mountain, where the skiing is.

Kitzbühel (opposite) is archetypical old ski town, set in valley, built in age-old peasant-village architecture. Town plan is medieval, fit for foot traffic. "Kitz" is famous for **its many great Austrian racers,** and its exuberance in celebrating formalities with town band (below). **St. Moritz (1)** is most sophisticated Swiss ski city. Other skiers take their sport in simpler places (below 1).

well as of all-cost-paid tours of the Black Forest, Oberammergau, and Mad Ludwig's castles. It's Hansel-and-Gretel land, where German Bavaria meets the Austrian Tyrol. Skiing is a recent upstart, even more so than in St. Moritz. Half the people here are hikers, riding the lifts and then hiking calf-deep in snow to one of the restaurants sitting on peaks around the town with an outdoor terrace and a view to please Goethe. D. H. Lawrence, living in Bavaria, wrote, "I think every hilltop in Germany over 2,000 feet high must be crowded with Germans stepping heavenwards."

Garmisch has traffic patterns, police at the corners, big hotel rooms with enough space around the beds for the whole family to practice barbells, a dozen of each kind of restaurant, a hundred *Bierstuben*, high-fashion shops at every intersection. Hard-goods stores sell intricate musical beer mugs, masterful wood carvings, serpentine smithy work in precious metals, and the ultimate in cuckoo clocks.

In the serious restaurants—and they are almost all serious—the cuisine is built around contempt for cholesterol. No one prepares veal so well as the Germans, and there are sixteen different forms of *Schnitzel*. The bread alone is a fragrant meal. The butter is exquisite. You haven't had a dessert until you've had Salzburger Nockerl, a rich foam of delectable stuff.

There is the veritable eyrie of skiing known as the Zugspitze outside town, where the European penchant for elaborate emplacements on inaccessible peaks reaches a dizzy zenith. The Zugspitze is the highest of the German peaks, circa 10,000 feet. The Germans have dug a complete hotel down into the mountain rock, the Schneefernerhaus, with dining room and white linen service, barbershop, and post office. You reach the place by a train which winds through a four-and-a-half-mile tunnel inside the mountain in security from wind, weather, and vertigo. Many ride, but few ski.

Enough of the cavalier attitude toward skiing. In the eastern third of Austria, the part of the Tyrol the Turks once ruled, is Kitzbühel, the largest Austrian ski town. Here skiing is the thing. It is the home of Toni Sailer (by any rational account the finest racer who ever lived), home of the Kitzbühlers who make up half of any good Austrian race team. This is the town from which, for many years, the Austrians ruled the race world.

Kitzbühel's highest peaks are only a bit farther above sea level than the pavements of the city of Denver. Kitz is not situated in extreme Alpine country. The snow has to be watched to see that it doesn't evaporate before you get there. But Kitzbühel is a marvelous town. The weather usually is beautiful and warm. Your long underwear may lie folded in your closet for weeks in the coldest months. When the wind clears the sky, the Tyrolean Alps seem to be white waves in the luciferous air.

The town is almost Hollywood-Tyrolean. Huge medieval (c. 1200) walls of heavy masonry circle the center of town. Inside the wall itself, shops and inns are built-in; the center of Kitz looks like an old print of the London Bridge. Within the town are small and large hostelries, on the order of castles and monkish inns. On the narrow streets Mercedes-Benzes move carefully through crowds of slick-panted girls and bronzed, good-looking men. French, German, and American accents mix.

There are 8,000 Kitzbühlers in town, and even at the height of the winter season they are not outnumbered. Kitz harbors bootmakers and tailors who build the best boots and cut the best ski pants in Christendom. The Kitzbühlers are the Red Devils of the ski school and the waiters and maître d's and the slap-kick-leather-britched *Schuhplattler* dancers, the zither players, the tea-room girls; there is a strong bias toward Tyrol. Everyone not Tyrolean is a tourist.

The girl tourists are young and beautiful, and they congregate at the Tenne, a rock-and-roll tea-dance palace at the venerable Goldener Grief (c. 1400). If you haven't made contact at the Tenne by the end of the tea-dance hour, you need to get yourself a pair of hand-tailored stretchpants and a good night's sleep.

It is not easy in Kitz to find one's proper level of skiing and after-ski. A couple of American girls I once overheard in the bar at the Praxmair expressed the opinion that if the skiing didn't get any better and the night life come alive, they were going back to Stowe, Vermont. They had spent their morning jarring their eyeteeth on frozen snow of the north-facing Streifalm (they should have saved that for warmer afternoon temperature), then trudged over to the other side of town and come down the south-facing Kitzbühler Horn when the late afternoon snow there, directly in the sun, was soggiest. They had gone straight to their pension, thereby missing the tea dance at the Tenne and their best chance for a date. Next they wandered morosely down to the teenybopper den at the Praxmair, which was too young for them.

Half of the good times at Kitz are on the hill—the multiplicity of hills which have to be skied at the right time of the day. The runs go to half a dozen towns around Kitz, and provide the added satisfaction of stopping at, or at least seeing, the mountain hotels that are set out on the *Alm* (Austrian for alp). There are no auto roads to the hotels, only sled tracks, but there they stand, each—typically—with a sun porch a mile long. Also in among the runs are small inns and beautifully built farmers' guest châlets. You continually ski past fancy sleighs carrying guests to on-the-mountain res-

taurants and inns. (The only independent, on-slope restaurants in the United States are one at Aspen and one at Taos.) Work sleighs driven by Kitzbühel farmers slog along, bringing hay bales from the hay huts to the cow barns. There are sled paths, walking paths, and ski runs intermingled and congruent. A run can dead-end ten miles from the walls of Kitz after you traverse a series of cow paths, farmers' fields, and wooded slopes. What do you do? Your guide calls a VW bus-taxi and you sit on the porch of a country inn, eat cured ham and drink fine beer until your taxi shows up.

St. Christoph is Austrian, too, but at the opposite end of Austria, a handful of buildings set at the top of the Arlberg Pass under the shadow of the Valluga. St. Christoph is opposite to Kitz in every respect. Kitzbühel is big and St. Christoph small; Kitz is low, St. Christoph high (8,750 feet); Kitz is rolling, St. Christoph precipitous; Kitz is east, St. Christoph west. The contrast is an analogue to eastern and western skiing in the United States. But the animosities between the Kitzbühlers and the Arlbergers are deep and grievous, far outrunning American prejudice. Even on the national race team, they keep apart.

St. Christoph is where you stay in the Arlberg if you really want to ski. For après-ski you stay down in St. Anton and suffer the additional lift-riding time to the top of the Valluga every morning.

The Arlberg is the cradle of the world's ski teaching. The famous Arlberg Club was formed in St. Christoph in 1901 to teach refined techniques of dragging the single six-foot ski pole as a brake. St. Anton is where the first of the world's great ski systems was born: the Arlberg system codified by Hannes Schneider. And in St. Christoph the current world master of ski teaching, Prof. Stefan Kruckenhauser, has his winter headquarters. He presented the reverse turn and wedel to the world of recreational skiing. The Arlberg terrain is the snobbiest region in the skier's world, in terms of skiing per se. On no other hill do instructors ski with

Gstaad, in Bernese Oberland of Switzerland, combines luxury and simplicity. The look of its picturesque châlets is enlivened by carved-wood exteriors; a single large hotel, the Gstaad Palace, stands at center of everything.

Traditional ski-country scenes abound in traditional Switzerland (clockwise from top): Embellished doorway at Klosters, ornate wall lamp in Palace Hotel at St. Moritz, overview of cozy village of Madrisa at Klosters; skiers wander among shops on narrow streets of Gstaad; flags of skiing nations fly every day at Mürren.

such rigid precision; on no other hill is your every turn monitored by so many eyes; on no other hill do the top classes get put through such awful snow and terrain.

Yvon Muret owns and runs Sportshotel Galzig in St. Christoph. Muret is French, yet has made a niche for himself through sheer skiing ability. If you think it is easy for a Frenchman to break into the Austrian instructor-guide world, then you know nothing about the French and Germans. Muret is probably fifty and can ski anywhere at any time in the maze of mountains and trails that swing down from the Valluga at the top of the Galzig cable from St. Christoph.

The Vallugagrat is a cliffside that either shatters you or sends an adrenalin high through your body, depending on how you feel about your skiing that day. I started off with Muret down the Vallugagrat one overcast day with fair to middling packed snow—no powder in sight. I made it down in about thirty-two turns out from under the cliff. Muret did about three sweeping turns. Before the day was over, Muret had found powder, somewhere, I can't remember exactly where, but in a deep hidden pocket back in the outermost reaches of the Arlberg Pass terrain. He also found us some breakable crust, some slippery wet snow, and lots of intermediate things. One of our group of four was a beauty from France. Her husband, who wasn't quite up to the rest of us in ski ability, surrendered at noon to take a taxi back from some small inn down the east side of the Arlberg. He was *kaputt*, perspiring and steaming. Game, but outskied. We went on. And on. I have never skied so far, through so intricate a series of passages, in so many different kinds of snow and over such a variety of terrain at so many different altitudes in so many different villages all in one day. I took out a map and traced the whole thing back with Muret's jocular help that night. We had skied, minimum, thirty-five miles, not counting turns. Just a normal day for Muret.

But there are not just old ski towns in Europe. There is a brand-new kind of ski town, as well. The

Arosa is one of four superlative resorts in the Grisons, Switzerland's largest canton, right next to Austria. As in others (St. Moritz, Klosters, Davos), accent is on cuisine, shops, après-ski, village color and ambience.

new skiing is in France. The different kind of ski town now being built there is centered on the "ski skyscraper," or "ships of the snow," as the French call them.

Private entrepreneurs have succeeded in producing in the French Savoie (a region that abuts southwestern Switzerland and northwestern Italy) a modern, sun-filled, surpassingly designed collection of ski villages. The magic names are Flaine, Avoriaz, Les Arcs, Tignes, La Plagne, Les Menuires, and Courchevel.

From Geneva, one memorable occasion, Bea and I drove with Peter Miller, who photographed the new French resorts for this book, to make our first round of the magic names, beginning with Flaine. Flaine is barely forty miles from Geneva. The other Savoie resorts are within three hours. (Imagine living in New York if Sun Valley were forty miles off, Vail fifty, and Aspen sixty. That's how Geneva looks from a skier's point of view.) In two hours, we were dropping down the S-curves toward Flaine at the end of a vertigo-inducing road. The valley of Flaine was uninhabited and uninhabitable five years ago, twenty impossible miles from any road, inaccessible, remote, inhospitable. "Let Flaine be," said France, and Flaine was.

Flaine is monumental, elemental, a restatement of the mountains. There were no bits-and-pieces of an old mountain village weathered in place. Flaine is set there by the hand of industrial man, a half-dozen severe eight-story buildings forming a square, out of which a soaring cable car rises.

Flaine is other-worldly, devoid of the traditional carved eaves and crooked streets. The lack did not grieve me. I had survived enough peasant ski villages to hold my enthusiasm for peasant decoration in check. Your farming village by mid-morning will often have an ungemütlich traffic jam. Your reservation is not to be found. You trudge from pension to pension to get rooms. One of the independently owned lifts around the town closes mysteriously at 11 A.M.,

just as you get there. After skiing, you have to replace a ski pole. You hunt around town for a ski shop in the slush on slick cobblestones, dodging deadly vehicular traffic (machismo rules the road). It's raining. You get back to the pension too late to change for the dinner dash. The nearest three restaurants are full. That's a ski village, tradition and all.

Flaine is another story. Here the supporting cadres are ready, the supplies are laid in and waiting, your apartments ready for occupation, your place in the dining room set. Three hotels—one, two, and three stars—connect by well-lit, inside passages to all you need: the drug store, the ski shop, the art gallery, the movie house, and most certainly the discothèque.

During our stay at Flaine's Gradin Gris (two stars) we had great food, fine wine. There was no where-do-we-eat problem. No car problem, no getting-to-the-shops problem, no getting-to-the-lift problem. No problems. Everything was right there, within a five-minute walk of any point. The French at Flaine have deftly extracted the thorns of the sport, of which there can be many.

This kind of resort obviously is expensive to build. The wonder was worked by credit from the local, regional and national governments. And they are built at the ideal location for skiing, which the traditional European ski village is not. An older European village is built in a sheltered location, surrounded by a ring of lifts, all a mile away. The new Savoie resorts are built in small, treeless, beautiful, distant valleys like Flaine, or on spectacular but restricted *balcons*, mountain ledges. The buildings are high and connected to offer strong protection against the sweep of the weather, which can be frightful down to 6,000 feet in the Alps, which is where the treeline begins in Europe. (In Colorado, it lies at nearly 12,000.) Thus, the new "ships of the snow" are anchored on ski terrain where only shepherds built summer huts before.

Les Arcs is far, far up a fantastic switchback road above Bourg St. Maurice, which used to be

Spectacular new directions
in European ski-town
architecture in the French
Savoie: Cluster housing on
a high plateau at Avoriaz
(r, above r, & opposite),
apartment tower in Les
Menuires (above), and high-rise
condominiums at Les Arcs
(below l). Circular staircase
graces hotel at Sestriere,
(below r), pioneer Italian resort
far ahead of its time.

classed as a ski resort. The Bourg St. Maurice cable runs no higher than the point at which the new skiing at Les Arcs begins. The skiing at Les Arcs is on bare mountain, under a blistering bright sun, with its poma lifts (invented by a Pole named Pomagalski) forming a spider web in typically French fashion, spreading onto the nearby peaks and into the valleys uphill, downhill, and around corners.

Louis Georges Joinon, the witty and traveled official greeter at Les Arcs, introduced us at lunch on a mountain to a charming French couple—both fellow journalists. Fearful that we would not find anything to write home about among the nine restaurants at Les Arcs (five in the village and four on the mountain), they took us to a small provincial inn of two tables in a village of about thirty houses. We had country-cured ham, salt olives, turnip strips, sliced potatoes cooked in buttermilk, fried thin beef slices, cheese, and an endive salad; we finished off with a light cake, with chocolate cream filling and fresh whipped cream on top. A local brandy and coffee. We tottered back to the car. The new resort, but the same old French.

The skiing towns of North America are fewer. Europe can boast a good fabulous forty, but the real ski towns in North America can be counted on the fingers of two hands: Stowe, North Conway, Franconia, Lake Placid, and Manchester in the East; and in the West, Sun Valley, Aspen, Steamboat, and Vail, with a few more coming into being slowly, but still not definite or complex enough or with enough of the St. Christoph kind of tradition to be considered *towns.* Places, yes. Not towns.

The towns of the American East, like those of the older European terrain, are outgrowths of farming communities. But American farming is a rather pallid newcomer, a bare two-hundred-year rather than a two-thousand-year enterprise. The American farm towns are ruder and the après-ski facilities similarly less well-established, less traditional, even spartan. In New England it's cold enough at a thousand feet above sea level to have plenty of snow most of the winter. The ski scene is spread through a lively, varied farm and forest country laced with cleared fields, ponds and family wood lots, red barns and old brick factories.

Skiing itself established a small foothold as a resort sport here in the 1930's, the Rooseveltian, post-Depression era. In contrast, there were well-established centers of sport skiing in Europe operating in the 1920's. St. Moritz had the first winter games in 1928. Lake Placid, New York, was host in 1932, but the contrast with St. Moritz is instructive. There was never established at Lake Placid variety of the sort seen at St. Moritz. The Olympics washed over Lake Placid and receded, leaving a slight impression. Nearly a generation after the Olympics, Lake Placid got a hill, Whiteface, with decent size to it.

There are other eastern conglomerations, such as Wilmington-Dover, that consist mostly of acres laid down in second homes, condominiums, and châlets, plus the steady speckling of inns and motels used by skiers. The same kind of sinuous strip-building along the roads that has ruined so many American towns, leaving them to rot at the center and grow randomly at the edges, has deprived us of the sort of concentrated ski town that Europeans have by the score.

A typical American non-town can be seen in the strings and strips of inns running from Rutland, Vermont, up toward Killington, currently the most enterprising of the Vermont resorts. There must be fifty places to stay scattered along the roads and not a decent village center. Killington is building itself a village at the foot of the mountain, with a concentration of shops and condominium apartments, but this is the first thought-out ski community in Vermont, and it's very new.

Waterville Valley in New Hampshire comes closest to the kind of thing that Europe has, but Waterville is also very new—mostly second homes with relatively few services and conveniences in place, certainly not the con-

In American West, ski towns often mix old-time false-front saloon architecture, as at Telluride (above r), with contemporary resort design utilizing tilted planes and periscopes, as at Squaw Valley, California (1), and Sun Valley's International Village.

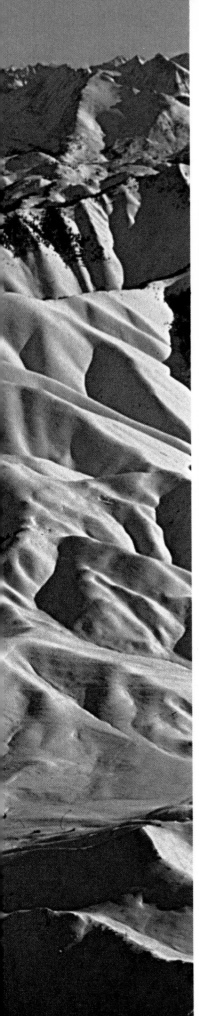

Sun Valley (opposite) began as neo-European ski village, but latest section (at right in picture) is typical U.S. châlet complex. Stowe, Vermont (top), is capital of northeast skiing. Keystone, Colorado (above l) shows new look. (Sign deters no one.) Aspen (l), an old Colorado mining town, is biggest ski village and cultural center in Rocky Mountains.

centration of people, shops, cuisine, and other accoutrements of good living that one has even in the new, instantly implanted French resorts.

The best of the old American ski towns in the East are plain, offering the joys of austerity. This is not said in any adverse spirit. Many of the happiest ski hours I've had have been there. The East is cold and stormy and moist compared to the West, or to the alps and alms of Europe; and the East's snow gets hard very fast. But the very best of old New England lives in the ski towns of the East. The people are pleasant. Your New England Yankee is one of the nicest people in the world to meet on a casual basis, combining a friendliness and a lack of obsequiousness that is unique. He can get along with you and he can get along without you, and neither bothers his even humor.

Stowe is the capital of Yankee skiing and the biggest ski town, the archetype. Stowe is neither an old resort town nor a newly emplaced ski village, but a resort displacing an older farming community that slowly turned to tourism as farm houses converted to inns. There is a "four corners" around which the ski inns of the town cluster. There are also lodges scattered for miles around on the roads and lanes. There are stores and services and restaurants in Stowe. It is surrounded on all sides by rolling hills, barns, corn-stubble fields, and winding brooks that run under the snow, sparkling through holes in the ice. Up on the mountain, a heavy pine forest forms the very matrix of the skiing, giving way to the second-growth hardwoods on the lower levels. Huge elms and oaks line the roads, and an occasional stand of white birch blends softly with the snow.

The older lodges are roughed out with minimum decoration, a plain and serviceable concept. (Wood is plentiful in America.) Typically a farm-converted-to-lodge comes simply furnished. It consists principally of the bedrooms and a sitting room or parlor and, if food is served, a rough dining room. There may or may not be a fireplace lounge.

The skier is the farmer's lodger rather than a tourist.

This motif is carried through even in the later lodges in New England, which tend to be a bit fancier. The mystique persists of the pilgrim settler without a farthing to waste on superfluities. There are, of course, luxury places in Stowe: the Lodge at Smuggler's Notch, Top Notch, and—in a different vein—the big, typical tourist motels. But there's a contingent of New England inns left to sustain the tradition.

New England skiing is based on the weekend. There is little midweek business even though the trend to winter vacations has begun to ameliorate the up-down syndrome. But part of the past for every skier in New England includes a long drive on the roads on Friday night, and the late arrival at the lodge, with a note left pinned to the outside door, "Mr. Lund, your room is second on the left upstairs."

In an old-style lodge, the skier is awakened early to breakfast, like the farmer getting to the morning milking. A very pale winter sun moving slowly heavenward; your host comes to the board tables with a steaming dish of oatmeal laced with brown sugar, smokehouse bacon coming up on a side dish and flapjacks and a jug of thick, brown, undiluted maple syrup. The breakfast sits in your stomach like a fireball exuding energy as you hurry out to rack the skis on the rime-covered car, snow creaking delightfully underfoot. It's twelve below. You have to beat the Saturday morning crawl to the lift—or you lose half a day. Coax the car to a roar of life; off post-haste to the Stowe single chair, the first chair in New England, and up the side of Mt. Mansfield, a wool blanket over your knees slowly admitting the cold, cutting sub-zero air that seeps past the protection of L. L. Bean's best long underwear. You know you have to move on that first run and you firmly deny the desire to collapse at the Octagon hut at the top to warm up.

The forest is a wonder of evergreen dipped in snow, and hardwoods with snow fingers; the trail is as hard to the skis as New England granite; keep clear of trees and shoot through the bumps to the safety of the runout. It's over. Your legs are like rubber. You have the cup of coffee and doughnut you promised yourself at the bottom. It's nine thirty.

The West: another country. Less harsh, drier and higher. Western ski towns are of two kinds: the artificial, emplaced towns that owe something to Europe, and the Wild West town, a kind of ski town that has nothing in common with anything else in the world.

The first and still the most redoubtable of the emplaced towns, Sun Valley, up in the Idaho Sawtooth, was America's first complete ski town, with the lift, lodge, and after-ski under one management, in this case the Union Pacific Railroad. The place was picked by Count Felix Schaffgotsch, a good friend of the railroad's president, Averell Harriman, who liked to ski.

Unfortunately, Count Felix put the village right in the middle of the valley, next to three small hills that, in those early days, satisfied everyone's thirst to ski. Today, of course, everyone buses three miles to Mt. Baldy, where there's real skiing. But Sun Valley, and western skiing in general, is a very relaxed sort of skiing, compared to the stern necessities of New England. The ski towns of the West are like Europe's vacation towns. People have more time and more money. It's warmer than the East, yet the snow is there to stay, from Thanksgiving to Easter, and won't go down the drain with a rain or two.

Union Pacific bore the losses of running a first-class European establishment in the middle of Idaho, where almost no one could get to it. Today the valley has changed. It is being built up by its new owner, Bill Janss. Condominiums are mushrooming all around the flats of the valley, bringing into being some contemporary American condominium architecture, all weathered woods and western-looking, but also making Sun Valley a much, much busier village.

Aspen is the best example of the Wild West ski town. It inhabits old Aspen, a sizable mining city in the late 1800's. The original Opera House, built for extravaganzas put on by silver-rich barons, still stands. The Jerome, a jewel of a Victorian hotel, still takes guests. The town is a wild ensemble of motel, Victorian villa, and slick condominium lodges. All told, the town's beds hold a good eight thousand visiting skiers.

Aspen and Sun Valley are the only American ski towns that have developed a thorough-going, self-sustaining culture of their own, a sort of out-West skiing version of the Beautiful People. The style captured Aspen before it spread to the rest of the country: the beard, the offbeat clothes, the casual bright hippie-cum-flower-people-cum-entrepreneur kind of look.

Aspen practically invented that great American, the ski bum, but it is getting harder and harder to bum in Aspen. More and more people want the Aspen life. There are several honest-to-God aging millionaires teaching in the Aspen ski school. The life style is the best, and really you don't need all that much money; just some earnest scrambling. By the time winter has come, every scarce room at reasonable rates has been fought for and divided up, and every scarce job landed by girls in granny glasses and guys with mustaches.

These beautiful bums can ski. They also have a strong hand in running Aspen's town government, equal to that of the hotel owners, entrepreneurs, and the ski corporation. The resident popular vote has managed to legally discourage the kind of three-hundred-percent expansion that has hit Sun Valley.

Aspen après-ski is absolutely great. There are a dozen excellent bars, some in flawless Victorian character, a handful of outstanding restaurants, and six or seven rock dance parlors, half of them disappearing and being replaced by others every year.

Good-looking girls, girls, girls, girls; cool men to match. A big town for swinging. A town to make it big in: Aspen, the Big Apple of American skiing.

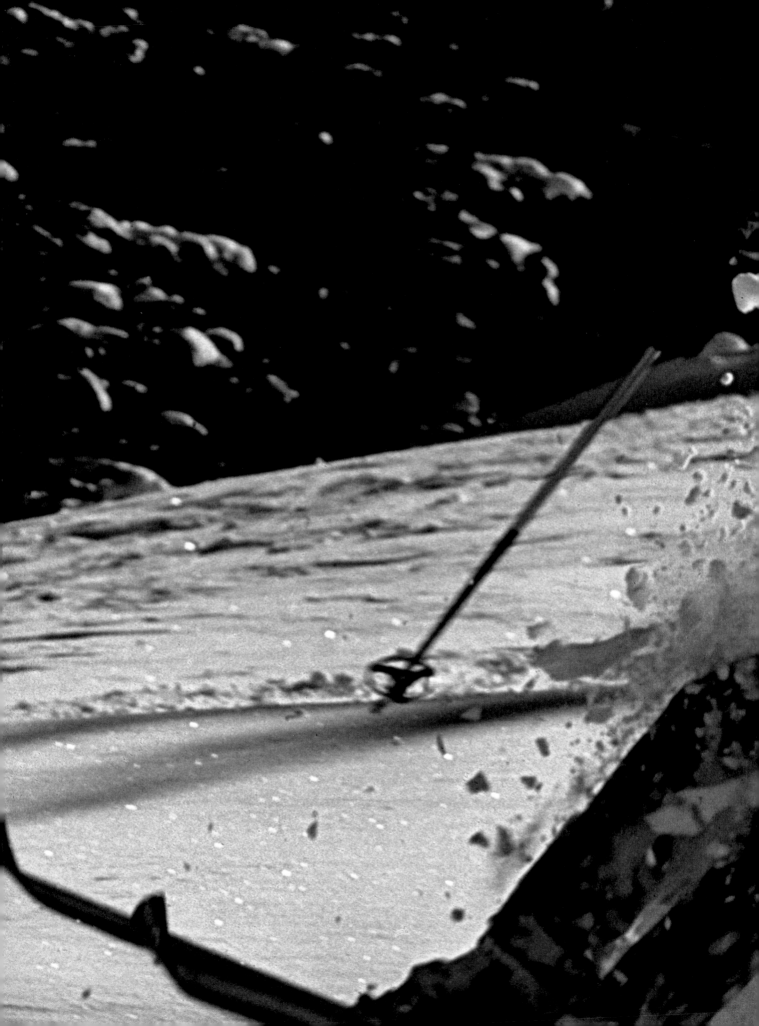

4

Man has a drive, perhaps one with survival value, to alter his state of consciousness from time to time. Small kids whirl to make themselves dizzy; dervishes dance themselves into a religious trance; teen-agers drag race. All of them alter their perceptions by subjecting themselves to unusual motion and thereby induce an unusual, altered state of consciousness. Thus a definition of the psychology of skiing: an unusual state of consciousness induced by an unusual, fast, sliding motion over snow.

It's interesting that the straight-down slide, "Schuss," comes from the German *Schuss*, or "shot," because the sensations of speed are somewhat similar. When you can slide at unusual speeds over a trail, you turn even a dull trail into excellent fun. The timing over each bump has to be right, the turns must be made deftly, and the body kept limber to counter the fierce swiveling rocking action of the skis, rattling over the small bumps and jolting upward over the moguls. A good schuss is a "high," a sustained rush of emotion, an unusual state of consciousness.

The racer is the disciplined example of the fast skier. In *The Ski Race*, an incisive movie made by Paul Ryan, a racer describes how he feels as he gets in the starting gate: "I am so wound up, man, that nothing matters but just to get down that hill. I can't think of anything but go, go, go."

Who wants this feeling? Everybody. Or at least every skier. To get it, he shrugs off the risk, forgets the hurt, the cold, the cost of weariness.

It is an acquired taste. My nephew Peter, age six, going up the beginners' T-bar lift at Sugarloaf, in Maine, rode between his father's legs. That went very well. On the way down, Peter fell several times. After his last fall, he said, "Dad, isn't there any way to get down but ski?"

Those of us who started skiing together in college in the forties are now looking at middle age. The one thing that makes us stay in shape is the haunting fear that, come winter, we won't be able to slide as fast as we thought we did last year.

I took up skiing in Maine at a time when the distinct difference between downhill or "sliding" skiers and cross-country or touring skiers was just beginning to develop. The catalytic agent of change was uphill transport. The first ski tows in this country were built when I was three or so, and the first skier-carrying lift (the chairlift at Sun Valley) when I was ten. Two years later the first big eastern lifts were installed at North Conway and Stowe.

The first uphill device I encountered was the rope tow. Today's skiers who never have had to "ride a rope" haven't missed a thing. Just one of the many troubles with a rope tow is that the rope itself is often so slippery you lose your grip and slide backward as the rope sandpapers a hole through your mitten. Or the rope is coated with freezing snow and your mittens adhere to it. One of my friends was lifted clear off the ground by such a tow. At the upper end he was almost carried into the pulley, which was suspended from the wall of a barn ten feet above the ground. He finally freed his hands from his mittens, which had frozen around the rope, and dropped to the snow. The mittens, still clutching his ski poles, went through the pulley.

The limitations of rope tows disqualified them from major impact on the sport. What was needed were long, comfortable lifts, so the skier could really learn to slide.

The first big lift in the East was the famous Skimobile that ran right straight up Mount Cranmore at North Conway. Its little wooden trestle carried an endless chain of vehicles the size of carnival bump-a-cars, traveling at ten miles an hour. To go that fast up the 1,500-foot vertical of North Conway—a hell of a vertical in those days—seemed like riding the devil's handcar to heaven. Minute by minute, the increasing pitch of the hill threatened to spill the whole car end over end down the trestle. Most of us who rode to the top had

SKIERS

little or no experience with a sizable ski mountain, but we went anyway, because the lift was there.

One time in the 1940's, at about my fourteenth fall on my way down Cranmore, a vision in a wide-visored cap came sailing over the slopes, a skier who seemed almost airborne. It was Hannes Schneider, doing beautiful parallel turns. Few skiers in those days had ever seen a parallel turn, much less attempted one. Today probably half the skiers on any given slope can "parallel" at least a little.

When I skied at North Conway in the late thirties and early forties, there were perhaps a dozen big lifts in New England. In the post-World War II era there were several hundred. The lift conquered the sport and made all of us sliders.

Lift riding became a separate game inside the sport in itself, a game most skiers play rather well. There was (and is) the battle of the lift line: to get your place and improve it. This includes tactics such as sneaking around to the inside of the turn and getting your ski tips in front of the guy in the next outside lane. The countermove is to put your pole down in front of the would-be lift-line passer in such a way that the basket catches the point of his ski, rendering him unable to proceed. Part of the battle is getting the right partner for the ride up, avoiding the old bores with gray hair, concentrating on the young, nubile, or handsome types. Much to be said here, but the rules become obvious.

There is a style to riding a chairlift, casual ways to show you are a good skier. The poles go under the legs and the skis dangle, decoratively, making daffies with an exaggerated walking motion or snaking back and forth parallel, as if wedeling right down the middle of a trail. The skier on a T-bar or a poma lift can make a little wedel track just to the side of the main track up, and that is very impressive to the people coming up behind him.

The actual perils of lift riding are not negligible. About a third of the accidents in the sport occur on lifts. The very considerable literature on lift accidents compares favorably with that of train wrecks. There usually are fewer people involved in a lift accident, but the action can be quite spectacular. In a single winter at one area in Vermont, for instance, two lift-mechanism failures produced two hair-raising incidents. In the first, the brake on a chairlift failed. The chair line started to go backward much much faster than it had been going forward. Riders were in danger of getting thrown out of the chairs as they swung around the bottom bullwheel. This was averted by two quick-thinking attendants, who seized the occupants out of the chairs as they came past backward and hauled them to safety. "We were piling them up in the snow like cordwood," one told me later. There were only slight injuries.

In the second accident, another chair brake failed. The attendant at the top jerked the emergency brake. The sagging cable between the high lift towers was pulled taut, catapulting the skiers out of their chairs and into orbit, so to speak, and then parabolically back into the snow. Luckily, only one skier was really hurt.

Lift accidents can be the result of unforeseen, unknowable problems, carelessness, or outright dangerous practices. It takes a capacity for infinite pains to make lifts safe. An overwhelming percentage of ski resorts measure up. A few don't.

Lift failures can be tedious rather than dangerous. Sometimes a chair lift will stop and won't go up again for a couple of hours. The problem is to get the people off before they get too cold. The usual solution is for the ski patrol to throw a line over the cable near a stranded chair and haul a little platform up to the chair. The skiers buckle in on the platform, and the patrol lowers them to the ground.

In all skiing, the accident rate has been going down, but it still runs around one-half of one percent per day. That means that out of a thousand skiers on a given hill, one will be hurt badly enough to need medical atten-

Opening pages: Bursting through crust, a skier in a modern sit-back stance makes turn with assurance in rough snow. Top recreational skiers today ski comfortably in tough conditions that would have stymied them a decade ago.

Four elements of style:
Corky Fowler (above) in the
stunt skier's classic
gelandy tuck; girl racer
(above r) takes skating
step to get right line for
next gate; Stein Eriksen (r)
demonstrates an extreme
"Austrian reverse." Skier
at Stowe (opposite) makes
typical square-shoulder wedel
turns while "walking"
his poles down the slope.

At Vail, Colorado, Jerry
Muth goes over a high cliff,
while Bob Burns uses avalement
in big moguls on Tourist Trap.
In differing situations, both
utilize sit-back for more
stability, longer recovery time
if skis catch, and more safety
provided by raised ski tips.

tion—a little or a lot—by the end of the day. It's a rare day at a big resort when there are less than two or three skiers riding the Ski Patrol's toboggan down the mountain.

Whenever the snow on the trails is icy and hard, paradoxically, the accident rate is lower. (Skis don't catch in the hard-packed snow so easily.) After a snowfall of nice, soft stuff, the accident rate zooms. There have been numerous soft-snow days at Aspen and Sun Valley that have produced a dozen broken legs.

There is competition among young orthopedic surgeons to get assigned to ski-resort hospitals. Not only can they ski on their day off but, more important, they will see more action during working hours than at any other location in the country. Skiers have advanced the science of orthopedics considerably in the United States.

Every skier sees the casualties. Skiers keep skiing even though there are people obviously being hurt all the time. Skiers, then, are a group of otherwise rather ordinary people with considerable *sang-froid*, betting that their own agility will see them through. Skiers are the only large group of adults who regularly risk this much. Sliding is so fantastic.

Most skiers are determined not to let the accidents—their own or others'—deter them. On one of the bad days in New Hampshire, a girl I was skiing with ran off the trail into a felled tree and wound her leg around it. We got her to the Franconia Hospital, and then we went back skiing while she was coming out of anesthesia. It is part of the therapy for survivors to get back on the snow again right away.

Fortunately, a preponderance of falls are not injurious. There are three kinds of falls: the safety sit-down, which even expert skiers indulge in from time to time; the sideways spill, "catching an edge"; and the boots-over-teakettle kind of spill where you are completely out of control. The latter either ends quickly in a smashing thump between the skis that literally takes the breath away, or it con-

Skiing is happiness:
Short skis, long skis,
standing on the tips,
skating alone, taking it
lying down, or skiing
in tight formation—skiers
find nothing comparable
to skiing for leaving the
rest of the world behind.

tinues quite a way down the slope. Then it's called an "egg-beater," or a "c-and-b"—crash and burn.

The sit-down can be quite artistic, a sort of swiveling slide into home plate. *Honi soit qui mal y pense:* Let him be ashamed who ridicules a thoughtful slide. Properly executed, the slide can blend into a neat rise to the feet while still underway—a cause for congratulations.

Probably the best and fastest getter-upper who ever lived was the late Olympic racer, Bud Werner. He recovered when others would have given up. In one qualifying race for the Olympic team, when he took a sit-down on a turn in the slalom and bounced up without losing a bit of headway, another competitor said, "Werner is the only man who can gain a second in a fall."

Another time, in a more serious fall, Bud disappeared in a cloud of snow halfway up the course. He emerged, jumping clear of the snow cloud before it had even started to settle, turned himself in the air like a cat, and went gunning down the course again. Unfortunately, he had broken a ski tip, so the recovery was in vain.

Falls can be accelerated by slick ski clothes. A slick jumpsuit on a slick slope equals acceleration. My wife once went down on the upper part of the National at Stowe while wearing a new yellow jumpsuit. Unable to stop, she went over three or four moguls, gathering speed and hitting each one harder. I skied behind, urging her to get her skis dug into the slope. She finally did and came to a stop, quite put out with her outfit. The later slick suits have nubs or ridges sewn in them to slow you down in a fall, a very salutary idea.

The most embarrassing kind of fall is into deep soft snow. The snow around the bottom branches of an evergreen tends to stay soft and loose, "bottomless." The unlucky skier who hits an evergreen can drop from sight and be unable to dig out because of his awkward position and the lack of support from the snow.

It's a very good idea never to ski alone on big terrain. Ravines and gullies can be very tricky. I lost a ski once over the side of Riva Ridge at Vail, and had to go down into a gully to retrieve it. Down was easy. Up was something else again. I found the snow on the sides of the gully so unstable that I simply couldn't climb out. The snow slid back as fast as I climbed out. I had to slog down the ravine bottom for fifty yards before I could find stable snow.

Once at Chamonix on the Grands Montets, my wife had to steer over a drop to avoid a novice skier who turned out in front of her. The drop-off went into a gully about twelve feet deep, and the snow was loose. Bea tried to climb out of the gully. For every step up, her skis slid back an equal distance. She waved to the people going by on the trail and shouted in French. They stopped, looked, and waved back. After half an hour, she took off both skis, and using the tail of one as a shovel, dug steps up the twelve feet and got back on the trail.

At the risk of some spectacular falls, there are all kinds of things you can do if the ordinary risks of sliding pall. There are moguls to jump, aerial splits to make, schusses to take, and rough snow to hit. And there are wild techniques to pursue. The new generation of hot-shot sliders have a sit-back style, *avalement*, and a "kangaroo turn" (turning on the tails) that looks like a backward fall minus the final thud.

There's a technique for moguls that calls for skiing partially out of control—"mogul bashing." The mogul basher skis *avalement* down the middle of the mogul field and at each mogul picks his skis up under him, so close under that his body continues in a level trajectory, skis smacking mogul after mogul with audible impact. It's an awe-inspiring way to get down the hill.

There also is mogul jumping. A good mogul jumper has to have faith plus a good steep runout to dissipate the kinetic force of the landing. My college roommate, an excellent jumper when he was young, happened across a kid[...]mp, barely a couple of feet high, and took it for fun. Bu[...]utjumped the hill and landed on the flat, breaking both anl[...]on the spot, thus ending his jumping career. The mome[...]n of the human body in a free fall is enormous.

The younger you are, the easier it is to [...]e faith. At every ski resort there are a number of natural mo[...] jumps where the kids congregate to wait their turn. Th[...]is an ethical question here, of course, of not running into no[...]mpers. So there should be—and usually is—someone do[...] at the landing spot, raising a pole to signal all is well, or cr[...]ng his poles overhead to show there are skiers coming. W[...] the coast is clear, six, seven, eight bodies go flying out ov[...]the slope, one after the other, hobgoblins riding the air an[...]isappearing down the trail so they can get back to their ju[...] as quickly as possible.

Barry Stott, an especially skilled skiin[...]hotographer, had a special jump spot halfway down S[...]ce Peak at Stowe. It was a beautiful roll that would throw y[...]ome distance down the slope. On one occasion Barry and a [...]end waited for all the skiers to go by to be sure the trail w[...]clear. The friend took off first for the roll. As he rose in the a[...]e started to make frantic motions and upon landing skied s[...]ght down the trail looking neither left nor right. On the d[...]n side of the roll, an entire, hitherto invisible ski class of e[...]t or nine people and the instructor were lying where they h[...] flung themselves in the snow to avoid the flying object.

That brings us to skiers as students. S[...]ing has a long history of schools and teachers.

The Norwegians exported sliding to [...]rest of the world, and the best skiers in Norway came from [...]emark. Here, by mid-nineteenth century, rudimentary forms [...] downhill sliding technique had differentiated themselves [...]m the rest of cross-country technique. The easy downhill [...]s called *slalom*. This comes from two words in the Telemark [...]lect, *sla* meaning "slack" or "easy," and *laam* meaning [...]ack." Slalom was fit for women and children.

The men's race was called *uvyrd-slaam*. *Uvyrd* means "wild" in the sense of going fast. In uvyrd-slaam the track went over drop-offs and down steep chutes. In one early uvyrdslaam, Sondre Nordheim, the best of the Telemark skiers, was said to have sailed more than a hundred feet in the air off one of the cliffs on the track.

The Norwegians not only were first to institute specific downhill sliding races, but they permanently advanced the art of making skis and bindings. The early flat, thick skis and over-the-toe thongs gradually evolved into a sophisticated slim-waisted ski better fitted for downhill sliding, and heel bindings that could be used to firmly direct the skis.

The Norwegians also invented the first downhill sliding turns. Before 1850, a ski turn was a sort of contrived accident, an attempt to "step" the skis to a new direction while underway. Then, Sondre Nordheim produced bindings that allowed the skier to turn the sliding ski without stepping it. At the same time, Nordheim fashioned a much more easily turned ski, one that had a great deal in common with the modern downhill ski: shorter, thinner, tougher, and more manageable than the wide, thick, seven- to eight-foot-long "transportation ski" commonly in use. Nordheim's binding aligned the foot more firmly with the ski. As the foot turned, it exerted turning leverage on the ski so that it was unnecessary to lift the ski to turn it.

By 1860 the best Telemark skiers had taken advantage of Nordheim's technology to develop the first precise ski turn, the "telemark." The skier went into a "lunge position" (like a fencer's), one foot forward. He actively swiveled the forward ski in the direction he wanted to turn. The rear ski, being on the inside, with the tip resting against the forward boot, was "herded" around the turn. The wide, lunging stance gave the skier stability in a fore-and-aft direction. The telemark turn could therefore be carried through in rough snow and over bumps. There was also side-to-side sta-

Skiing, also, is courting disaster. Even the best "crash and burn" once in a while (opposite). For the jaded, there's rock skiing (above) at Telluride, crevasse-leaping at top of Oregon's Mt. Hood (l). For that extra little jolt, one can trigger avalanches, like Tom LeRoy (below), and have fun beating them to the bottom.

bility. The inside boot was at least a foot to the inside of the turn. The telemark quickly demonstrated that it could be depended on.

The informal meets of the 1800's were not sharply differentiated into cross-country, jumping, and downhill. There could be a run combined with a jump on the way down. Later in the century jumping became a little more formalized. The outruns of the jumps were packed smooth, and Nordheim worked out a braking maneuver now credited to the alpine countries generally. This was the "snowplow," a means of slowing down in the outrun of a jump on hard-packed snow. In a snowplow, the tails of both skis are pushed out to the side and tips are held together in the middle. The skis are tilted, each at its inner edge; snow accumulates as before a snowplow and imparts a braking action. This was the first packed-snow turn and is depicted in a Norwegian ski manual published in 1888.

And, finally, the Telemarkers invented a third kind of turn, generally credited to the skiers of Christiania, the capital (later called Oslo). But it was the Telemarkers who developed what later became known as the "christiania." The tip of ski on the inside track of the turn was split away from the tip of the outside ski. The skier gradually shifted his weight to the inside ski. The term today for such a turn is "hooking," or "open christie," or "scissors christie." In point of fact, it is used "unconsciously"—almost invisibly—by a great many skiers to start parallel turns. It is a turn that comes naturally.

Christiania in 1866 began a series of annual city championships at Iverslokken near the old Akers church. The judging in those days was not based on time, but on the magnificence with which the contestants skied. Since the telemark was sweeping and theatrical, and the christiania sort of a crabwise skidding, Telemark wiped out Christiania.

That would have been the end of the christiania, except that the telemark is a "steered," long-radius turn, a turn with almost no slippage. The christiania, by contrast, is a sliding, short-radius turn with lots of slippage, involving a weight shift from one ski to the other, a turn rather more effective on the packed slopes encountered in modern skiing. So the "christie," as it's called today, is still with us.

By the end of the 1880's, Norwegians had demonstrated their plows, telemarks, and christies almost everywhere in the Alps. An engineer from Norway named Lindholm helped start skiing in Württemberg's Black Forest, which led to the forming of the Black Forest Ski Club. Another imported by the town fathers to teach skiing came to Kitzbühel. Another Norwegian, Nansen, wrote a book on skiing across the Greenland ice cap, and inspired the Swiss to found Ski Club Glarus, the earliest in Switzerland.

Where Norwegians failed to penetrate, the English took over and showed what they had learned from them. The foremost British promoter of skiing was Sir Arnold Lunn in Mürren, where his father owned the big resort hotel. Sir Arthur Conan Doyle, who pursued the mysteries of skiing, spiritualism, and crime with equal ardor, skied from Davos to Grindelwald in 1894.

Now we come to a pivotal figure in teaching sliding: Mathias Zdarsky, an officer of the Austrian army. He also was inspired by Nansen's book and sent to Norway for a pair of skiis when he retired to his home in Lilienfeld, west of Vienna. He took up skiing in earnest, and managed to produce two new kinds of sliding turns. Zdarsky found that if the tail of only *one* ski was "stemmed" out to the side, that ski would turn the whole skier more handily than stemming two skis, as in the plow turn.

Zdarsky later did even better. He found that if the second ski could be quickly brought around in a position *parallel* to the stemmed ski, the turn could be finished in a sliding turn, like the christiania. This turn provided superior braking. Both skis slid forward and sideways. Braking action was applied by two skis instead of one. Thus, the stem

Extra dimension of challenge
is donned along with the
racing bib. But to go as fast
as you planned does not
always lead to really happy endings.
Bucky Kashiwa contemplates
error of his ways and
a possible soft landing spot.
(He brought it on himself!)

christiania, or stem christie, was born. It was not a modern stem christie by any means. In Zdarsky's stem christie, the weight stayed on the inside ski (a great deal like the old early open christie). But the turn established the effectiveness of the parallel sliding position for the first time in ski history.

Zdarsky ran a school for Austrians—mountain troops and assorted skiers—at Lilienfeld, starting in 1892. His influence on Austrians was tremendous; he laid the groundwork for Austrian supremacy in ski racing that lasted until the middle of this century.

It took another Austrian army man, who sometimes worked with Zdarsky, to correct a couple of Zdarsky's anachronisms in ski technique. Col. Georg Bilgeri got Zdarsky to drop one-pole braking to the inside of the turn in favor of two poles, as the Norwegians had been doing ever since 1887. Unfortunately, neither Zdarsky nor Bilgeri adopted the Norwegian's upright stance, so the Austrian-dominated world of ski teaching was afflicted with the forward crouch for another generation.

Zdarsky hadn't entirely given up on the use of the pole for braking. His school at Lilienfeld considered fast sliding *gefährlich*. Better you should take both poles in one hand and use them like the old alpenstock brake, or, *in extremis*, they could be shoved between the legs and levered into the snow, so the skier rode the slope like a witch. It was not a fast technique, however. When Zdarsky was challenged in Austria to race a young Norwegian Telemarker, he was beaten badly.

Now appeared the famous Hannes Schneider. He was a Steuben-am-Arlberg boy, befriended and taught to ski by a man named Victor Sohm, who had studied with Zdarsky. Hannes' father wanted his son to be a cheesemaker, but Hannes applied to the Hotel Post in St. Anton to fill the newly created position of hotel ski instructor. He got the job. Hannes then worked out the brilliant notion of organizing his clients into structured class levels, so that as they

Concentration is needed to fly fast. It's needed by racer to take a big bump in good control (opposite), and by member of K-2 ski team (top). Only thing worse than disaster is not being daring enough, thereby losing altogether (above).

progressed they moved up a "ladder," unhindered by slow learners on the lower rungs. The "teaching ladder" has been with us ever since.

Schneider's steps for the ladder were the snowplow, stem, stem christie, and later, when it became teachable, the pure parallel turn. Schneider's ladder thus was a paradigm of the evolution of turning on skis. Only the telemark turn was dropped. Skiers had begun to use a stiff heel spring, which made it hard to raise the heel for a good telemark.

The difference between Zdarsky and Schneider was one of speed. The higher the speed, necessarily, the longer the slide. Schneider was so good at stem christies that he went to St. Moritz and beat the best Swiss skiers in a downhill race, using stem-christie turns against their telemarks. A telemarker had beaten Zdarsky, but Schneider beat the telemarkers.

Schneider's fame as a racer and his success as a teacher erased the stiff, slow stem christie, and emphasized the fast sliding part. In Schneider's technique, the stem part was only a beginning movement to get the turn started and the advanced stem christie was ninety percent sliding with skis parallel.

Enter now another key figure in the evolution of technique, a younger contemporary of Schneider's: Tony Seelos, the first Austrian superskier. Seelos was the first skier to make high-speed parallel turns on steep terrain. He simply dispensed with the initial stem movement and substituted a small hop, after which he came down sliding both skis together and continued the turn in a full slide. This was called "pure christie," or "parallel christie." The elimination of the stem eliminated the awkward braking action at the beginning of the turn, but allowed you to brake artfully toward the end. Seelos beat his competitors by ten seconds or so in races of the mid-1930's. The French team hired him to coach them. The star of the team was Emile Allais, who subsequently founded a French national teaching method based on the pure christie.

Schneider, on his part, simply incorporated the parallel as the top rung of his ladder. Schneider's pupils reached this pinnacle of sliding rung by rung. This was the Arlberg method.

In the late 1920's and early 1930's, the teachers of the Arlberg system invaded the United States to teach Americans skiing: Schneibs, Rybizka, Foeger, Ruschp, Lang, Matt, Buchmayr, Pfeiffer from Austria; Prager, Iselin, Thorner, and Loosli from Switzerland. Almost no one came from France in those earliest days.

In 1936, Otto Lang published the first book of technique for Americans, *Downhill Skiing*. He revised it in 1946. In the interim, the father of modern skiing himself, Hannes Schneider, displaced from St. Anton by Hitler's *Anschluss*, managed to escape to America to begin the Hannes Schneider Ski School next to the Skimobile in North Conway.

Lang's 1946 version of *Downhill Skiing* was a primer of the Arlberg method a generation ago: ". . . all the motions which the beginner will employ in his higher speed turns are incorporated in the basic snowplow turn. The goal is to lead the pupil as rapidly as possible but with safety, toward the stem christiania, the most universal turn in the advanced skier's repertory . . ."

And again: ". . . parallel christianias . . . cannot be taught in easy lessons: they can be acquired only through years of practice and experience as a skier."

All of us 1940 skiers learned parallel, rung by rung, after years of plugging. *If* we learned it. Today's younger skiers face a world bettered by several recent revolutions in sliding technique and teaching method.

During World War II, ski teaching methodology virtually stood still. Lang's 1936 book and his 1946 revision are much alike. Here's what Lang said in 1946 about the racing turn: "Just after you have reached the highest point of your elevation and your body begins to dive forward . . . the ends [tails] of the skis leave the snow and the skier virtually balances himself on the tips. This fascinating phenomenon of a

Learning: Old-fashioned
way is with long skis and
snowplow turn (top). Current
way is to use short skis
and make parallel turns right
away (middle l & bottom l).
You also can learn tricks
(middle r). Youngest may forego
putting on skis at all.

skier dancing on the tips of his skis can often be observed in a slalom race."

But in the early 1950's, Prof. Stefan Kruckenhauser, an Austrian physical-education specialist, the very model of a modern investigator, took high-speed films of the world-champion Austrian racers going through slalom gates. He went over the film prints slowly with a viewer and found that the standard Lang conception of the racing turn had been—gradually, unwittingly—set on its head.

Peering through his viewer, Kruckenhauser discovered that racers were no longer "elevating," or hopping up, as they had done when parallel turning first began. Instead they were *dropping down*. Kruckenhauser forthwith formulated an entire new teaching method that emphasized

"down-unweighting" and twisting the skis during the fraction of a second of weightlessness resulting. He called it the "heel-thrust." The practice of down-unweighting while quickly fanning the tails of the skis to one side produced a quick, sharp, short parallel turn without the necessity for an upward leap, or elevation.

    A heel-thrust in one direction and a heel-thrust in the other produce two quick parallel turns, drawing an elongated S-shaped track as the skier descends. It is perfect for a zigzag slalom racing course. The double heel-thrust, repeated, produced a series of short, connected, dance-like turns which Kruckenhauser dubbed *wedel*, from the German word meaning "to wag," as a dog wags his tail. Wedel is a powerful way to control speed down the steeper slopes and it

As day wanes, there
is blessed rest, luxurious
conversation, the company
of peers, sun-tanning in
splendid solitude or en masse
on the slope. After a last
stretch, as at Crans-Montana
in Swiss Alps, there's that
long, languid run down.

ultimately brought high-speed steep-slope skiing within the reach of good skiers, a new phenomenon.

In the 1950's, wedel was still restricted to the very advanced skier. At a meeting of the Professional Ski Instructors' Association in the middle 1950's, only three or four of the country's top ski-school directors could wedel, much less teach it. Wedel was taught *after* parallel.

Kruckenhauser's book, published in 1957 and translated in 1958 by Roland Palmedo as *The New Official Austrian Ski Technique,* was a full exposition of wedel. Its one fault: It was not focused enough on the precise leg motions of the connected heel-thrusts in wedel. This motion was called "leg play" *(Beinspiel)* and left at that. It took a further analysis of the wedel by Willy Schaeffler, the coach of Denver University, Mikki Hutter, an Austrian who was a top instructor, and me in *Sports Illustrated*, in 1959, to produce a more precise way to impart wedel at the intermediate level. Even so, we all missed giving the needed attention to the initial propeller-like rotation of the skis by the feet and legs.

Now occurred an entirely new revolution in ski teaching. Behind the revolution was Clif Taylor, a part-time instructor out of Brattleboro, Vermont. Taylor made the first usable short teaching ski.

To slide a ski into a turn is to overcome the resistance of the ski to being turned. This resistance is proportional to the square of the skis' length. The resistance of a six-foot ski has a factor of 6×6, or 36, compared to 7×7, or 49, for a seven-foot ski. To go in the other direction: A five-foot ski has a turning-difficulty factor of 5×5, or 25, a four-foot ski 4×4, or 16, and a three-foot ski 3×3, or a resistance of 9. Thus a three-foot ski has only one-fifth the resistance of a seven-foot ski to being turned on the snow. A three-foot ski? That's where Taylor arrived after a couple of years of experimentation. He found that, first of all, a properly designed three-foot ski could be skied quite satisfactorily at low speeds. (The average beginning skier almost never slides faster than eight miles an hour.) Furthermore, the skier could turn three-foot skis while standing still on them.

This led to the "Instant Parallel," or "short-ski method," practiced from 1957 to 1959 exclusively by Taylor at Hogback Mountain in Vermont, outside Brattleboro. The essential of the method was to get the pupils—lined up at a standstill—to practice turning their little three-footers underfoot, swiveling them like a metronome, in effect, back and forth, back and forth. The motion at a standstill supplied the ingredient that had been missing in early attempts to teach wedel to the average skier. All that remained to launch these beginners into a rough form of wedel was to start them doing the back-and-forth swiveling of the skis while going down a slope. Taylor proved that this was quite easy. Certainly as easy as teaching a snowplow turn. He had pupils skiing intermediate trails in a day.

Taylor's book, the first to analyze the method in pictures, was called *Ski In A Day*. The book showed that it was perfectly possible to start a pupil on three-foot skis, have him learn to turn them at a standstill, then turn them going down the slope, then progress to a four-foot ski, do the same sequence, and so on to a five-foot ski, and then onward to just as long a ski as the skier felt comfortable handling. As the length of the ski increased, the ski had to be held flatter and flatter to start the turn because the resistance of the ski to being turned was increasing as the square of the length of the ski. It was the first escape from the "historical-evolutionary ladder" method of teaching. But it worked.

Taylor's revolution did several things in a technical sense. It focused the attention of the instructor on the essential, that is, the swiveling of the lower part of the body turning the ski. Second, Taylor introduced short, connected turns at the beginning. Connected turns are the ideal way to control speed on a steep slope. Continual motion is also important in terms of keeping the skier relaxed and balanced, just as it is in riding a bicycle.

Naturally, the new concepts involved were difficult for the average professional ski instructor to grasp. There was the horrendous idea of teaching wedel to beginners. There was the problem of supplying the three lengths of skis to the pupil. There was the really unnerving propensity of pupils for going down an intermediate trail on their own after a single day of skiing. Very upsetting.

The history of the short-ski method shifts now to Killington, Vermont, where the ski-school director, Karl Pfeiffer, was induced by *Ski* Magazine to try Taylor's method to see if his exceptional results could be duplicated. Pfeiffer worked with the method for a year, introducing modifications. He packaged it neatly into a five-foot ski-vacation week, so that you started with three-footers on Monday and were skiing five-footers by Friday, making parallel turns.

The story of the Killington experiment appeared in *Ski* in 1966, a collaboration of Karl Pfeiffer and me. To give the method a more descriptive name, I coined the phrase "Graduated Length Method," or "GLM" for short. It has stuck. The rest is history. Today there is GLM wherever you go. It took only about six years from the story's appearance in *Ski*; by 1972, schools in every section had GLM.

It would be nice if that were the whole story, but with every reformation there is a counter-reformation. This came in the shape of a second kind of GLM, quite different and with quite different antecedents. To go back a bit, the French ski schools had been following Allais' idea that it is best to go directly to parallel, a perfectly straightforward and very French exercise in logic, and a very French way around the disciplinary Germanic learning ladder. For a long time, however, the system really worked no better for the French than the Arlberg did for others. Then came wedel, and the French seized on it because they foresaw that here at last could be the magic key to the early teaching of parallel. They actually managed to do a great deal of work and had some success in this endeavor. But, the French methods, in spite of the fact that they got equal space in *Ski* and other ski publications, were not at all influential in American ski schools, where Austrian instructors, faithful to their national traditions, were in command.

It wasn't long before Austria was heard from. Kruckenhauser, working with classes of kids, and undoubtedly drawing on the French work, came up with *Schwups*, a sort of basic, not too precisely executed stem turn which would replace all the intricate plows and stems, and which would, in the French manner, introduce a kind of wide-stance parallel turn very early on in the skier's learning. The transition was the so-called "open stem" in which the skier opens the tips of the skis in the stem, getting them more parallel and shifting weight from one ski to another in a series of short, connected slides.

Jerry Muth of Vail brought the Kruckenhauser system to the United States and made it work in a big way at Vail. But Muth borrowed the GLM idea of short skis as well. Skiers at Vail began on five-foot skis, skiing a "wedge" or sliding snowplow, and often graduated to wide-stance track parallel on larger skis within a week. Muth called this ATM, or American Teaching Method. It did not stress graduating to longer skis.

ATM on five-footers is somewhat easier to teach in the heavier snow in the West, where the snow is dry and will not pack down as well as it does in the wetter East. The harder the snow is packed, the more easily it supports a short ski. So ATM is the predominant way of teaching skiing in the West. Some western schools use the older three-foot GLM quite well. Some offer both methods. In the final analysis, the skill of the teacher and *his* faith in the particular teaching system, whichever it is, produces the best result.

The two kinds, GLM and ATM, have become embedded in the Professional Ski Instructors of America methodology, with the result that Americans have become the most advanced of the world's sliding teachers.

5

You ski Europe because it's there. It's been there—as ski terrain—longer than any place else. Europe is where skiers were being lifted in luxurious glass-enclosed cable cars while Americans were still mastering the awful strains of the rope tow and the Japanese had not yet begun to ski. Cables and cog railways built in Europe so that stout Victorian summer tourists could see the view turned out to provide ski descents of a grandeur that hasn't been duplicated anywhere else in the world.

The Europeans have a head start on the world that can't feasibly be overcome. They have established a nonpareil network of lifts and, consequently, a bigger customer pool. If you exclude Scandinavia and Scotland, the part of Europe that contains the big centers of skiing is not much larger than New England. Within this territory are well over a thousand big lifts and seven hundred ski resorts.

Once I drove from Flaine in the Haute Savoie—about as close to the Atlantic as you can ski on the Continent—and in two days went 600-odd miles eastward across all of Switzerland and part of Austria to Kitzbühel—about as far east as you want to ski, unless you have an East European visa. I was never more than an hour from a major ski resort; I'd passed north or south of all the major ones in Europe.

Europe's mountains are fairly teeming with huge swinging cables, long, sinuous lifts, and a bewilderment of trails. The mountainsides connect. You can circle through Stuben, Lech, St. Christoph, and St. Anton without getting off skis. You can go from Avoriaz in France to Morgins in Switzerland. You can ride over the rim of the Alps at Chamonix to go twenty miles by lift and ski to Entrèves in Italy. The highest North American vertical is just over 4,000 feet. In at least a half-dozen places, European lifts give access to about 6,000 vertical feet. In sum, Europe's terrain is extraordinary—more extensive, less obvious, more varied and complex than elsewhere.

Europeans have run their cattle high in the hills at least since Roman days. The sides of the European mountains are their high pastures. (The word for high pastures is *alp* in Swiss, *alm* in German.) Entwined in their cowpaths, their farm-wagon tracks, their footpaths, peppered with hay huts, pasture shelters, hiking cabins, is the European ski terrain.

All Europe's mountains, below glacier level, are familiar ground to someone. But fly over Colorado or almost any other mountain country outside Europe, and you can see thousands of acres of lonely mountainside comprising almost a *terra incognita*. No one goes there, certainly not in winter. The same is historically true of the larger New England mountains. Who farmed Mt. Mansfield in Vermont before the famous single chair went in? Who pastured cows on the top of Mt. Pisgah, which became Mt. Snow, the world's most heavily skied terrain? Who climbed to the open fields on top of Sugarloaf in Maine to hay? Nobody.

American resorts are formally designed for skiing. Typically, an American ski area has well-defined trails; it has relatively confined, hard-to-get-lost-in terrain. The trails return to the same base. All the trails are tracked daily—if not by skiers, then by the Ski Patrol because even "closed" trails not regularly patrolled during the day are "swept" by the Ski Patrol at the end of the day. The Patrol has a circuit of phones along the trails or they have walkie-talkies in their pockets. In Europe, you may be on your own.

The uplands of Europe are almost dangerously penetrable. Once a lift is built to a peak, the trails, in effect, are already in place. These are not the trails a trail designer would logically have emplaced, but they are trails nevertheless—the old pasture and hiking trails—and they might as well be used, no? Some of them are extraordinarily rugged skiing. But there is almost no "wild" country in Europe except at the very tops of the mountains and on the glaciers. Elsewhere the trees have been thinned, brooks bridged, and brush

EUROP

cut. The glades have been graded by centuries of hooves traveling to and from pasture.

On my stay at Avoriaz, the ski-school director took a class for an *itinéraire*, or day's run. We started out down a rather steep wall on the side away from Avoriaz. The snow had not quite softened under the morning sun and it scratched like limestone. We skidded through some bushes, split the next clump of trees, made a sidehill traverse of about half a mile, plunged down into the woods again and over a three-foot blind drop. Two miles of ho-hum running through a stream valley, across a couple of pastures, through two sets of weathered farm buildings, then on, beside a lake. Arriving three hours later at a single café seven miles from the start, we called Avoriaz Ski School for the bus. We sat down in the café, had delicious hors d'oeuvres and good beer. That's a good European ski day. Nobody said a word about technique. We had had a trip, an excursion, an *intinéraire*. A new café. That was enough.

This longish run was called *Piste* (the universal European word for trail) *du Lac.* Classed intermediate. That does not mean that the intermediate skier would *like* it, which would be the U.S. meaning, but that an intermediate could get down if he didn't scare easily, didn't mind scrambling a lot, and had blind faith he'd come out alive.

Your European guide-instructor *may* be paternalistic, and he may not. I have seen instructors shrug when someone can't handle the terrain. They are not callous. The European feels that once you have the stem turn, there isn't much one can do to improve except watch how the guide skis and pray fervently for the hand of God to put you in the ways of the stem christie and the saintly parallel. On the average, Europeans do not ski as well as Americans.

Even good ski teachers in Europe do not necessarily feel they can *talk* you into skiing better. An American, accustomed to the pleas of his American instructors (even Europeans teaching over here seem to be more concerned with their pupils than they are in Europe) can be left feeling a little deserted.

I had this feeling acutely when one teacher in St. Anton said to me, "If you want to ski powder, you must stop that silly nonsense of falling down."

Courchevel first, then four other Savoie resorts—Val d'Isère, Flaine, Les Menuires, La Plagne—have the best-groomed trails I've seen in Europe. Emile Allais' influence is very heavy in the Savoie. (He also headed the ski school at Squaw Valley for years.) In much of the rest of Europe, grooming is left to traffic, natural processes of the snow, and patchwork by *pisteurs*, the trail crews.

Admittedly, there are places in Europe where the grooming is American-thorough. But in most places, Europeans do not have the machines, or the will, or the terrain suitable for grooming trails as they are groomed in the States. This can be disconcerting for the intermediate skier, especially on *intinéraires*. Unless he knows that the terrain where he is invited to go is well-groomed, the intermediate would be better off not going on *itinéraires*. The British or European intermediate, used to the rougher snow, and more securely planted in his stem turn, is likely to do much better.

In nearly every European resort, there are always some trails, but not necessarily many, that are good, smooth, intermediate terrain. The bigger the resort, the more intermediate terrain it will have. St. Moritz' Corviglia is great if you stay on the packed-out runs (do not wander into the unpacked sections). Klosters, Zermatt, the Parsenn, and Verbier in Switzerland, and in Austria, Kitzbühel, Kaprun (particularly in spring), Lech, and Zurs. Again, the latter is best in a class or with a guide. The Savoie, as noted, has special places very like the American model.

The American system of grooming is going to be widely copied in Europe, if only for the reason that, wherever it exists in Europe, it's popular even with Europeans. On the other hand, American-style bulldozer-

Opening pages: Mountains over Innsbruck, Austria, are typically European in breadth and openness. Low treeline exposes Europe's slopes, makes them peerless skiing. And there are sumptuous establishments; Europeans have built in their mountains for centuries.

Skiing has a holy place,
that around St. Christoph
in the Arlberg, terrain of
the first coherent
ski instruction, by Hannes
Schneider, and now
home of his successor,
Stefan Kruckenhauser.
Endless alps of Austrian
Tyrol (top) embrace this pass,
where history, terrain,
and ambience combine to
lure pilgrim skiers.

grooming can be a real killjoy as far as the expert is concerned. Aspen and Sun Valley habitués are up in arms as the takeover by the bulldozer proceeds to parts of Ajax and Baldy historically sacred to the good skier.

A clientele of expert skiers cannot alone carry a major resort, so the bulldozer becomes ubiquitous. Take heart, experts: In Europe there are ten thousand runs *al fresco*, the way God and the last snowfall left them, and that basically is the way they will continue to be to the delight of "powder hounds" who want their snow deep and the gunk experts who like it thick. Europe is good to experts.

The visitor to Europe sees almost immeasurable treeless slopes that dwarf anything even the American Rockies at their most magnificent can provide. The sweep of the European open slopes is ravishing. The snowfields beckon, and promise, and exhilarate. But the exigencies of the extensive open-slope skiing of Europe are somewhat escalated. Unless you have local knowledge or are a veteran high-mountain skier, you *must* follow the marked trail across the slopes, and that means the ski tracks and the trail signs.

The unmarked slope—it looks so inviting—can contain dangers that only a Haute Route-type would want to handle. And, there is no guarantee you'll be returned to the bottom of any lift if you leave the track. Finally, you can get avalanched off the beaten track.

The Corviglia at St. Moritz has as fine an intermediate terrain as anywhere in the world—a range of open slopes and a panoply of ski lifts on the south face of a ridge looking on the Engadine Valley. The top of the funicular, Piz Nair, leads to the roughly parallel lines of lifts on this south face, about a mile apart, each with a couple of obvious runs packed out on each side. There are catwalk trails between the lifts and signs in between to keep you on the catwalks.

On the vaster open terrain on all sides, being bypassed by thousands of skiers on the packed trails, are gullies with deeply drifted snow, never packed out, never patrolled. You could get stuck in one of these gullies until dark, when they come up looking with St. Bernards. And there are a couple of headwalls that slide occasionally. Not big slides, but big enough to trip you up and cover your head with snow, which can be lethal if no one else is around.

In Europe, "open" means only "open where tracked." You are legally liable if your own tracks lead others into danger zones in Switzerland.

American resorts are constructed on combinations of the "diamond pattern," where trails diverge at the top of the hill, go out to a wide "waist" toward the middle elevations, and then turn back to meet at the lower elevations where the lift begins. Americans can do this because they unfailingly build in nearly virgin terrain; no alms, alps, or cowpaths, maybe a logging road or two, or a mine operation, but basically *tabula rasa*, a blank sheet on which a logical system can be easily drawn. In Europe, it's too late for logic.

From St. Moritz' Piz Nair, you can ski over the far side into the nice, gentle, rolling Saluver Valley, which happens to be there. But, if in the valley you miss the Marguns lift, you will have to go all the way to the village of Celerina. That is a run of about four miles—a bit too long for an intermediate unless he has all day to do it. At Celerina, if the cable to St. Moritz is closed, you take the bus back, of course, whenever that runs.

Visible across the Engadine Valley from the Corviglia is the Corvatsch, a peak with a skiable 5,800-foot vertical (three Stowes, or two Aspens, piled one on top of the other). The average run down is six miles long. You never see a tree until the last mile. The run itself can be done by an intermediate who knows the right turns to take. In my avidity to ski an honest 5,800-foot vertical, I tackled the Corvatsch alone one day when I was no better than advanced intermediate and, while I got down the whole thing without

so many tourists ski Austria.

Austria is where they invented having fun at skiing. They invented the ring *(circus)* of lifts, so you can always ski in a warm exposure; they invented the mountaintop sun porch, so you can tan while lunching; they invented the ladder-system of ski classes, so you can learn with equals; they invented the *Idiotenhügel*—the beginners' hill —so the novice won't be frightened by too much vertical, and the tea dance, so he won't be lonely for the evening. They invented the noodle, the nockerl, and the wurst, so you need never go hungry. They invented the inexpensive king-size hotel room so you can turn over expansively and "ski" in your sleep without crashing into a wall.

There is a kind of positive, good-natured drive characteristic of all Austrians I have known. I cite Willy Schaeffler, who came to America to become history's greatest college ski coach. He's not a terribly organized person, but he gives the impression of being very organized and induces a deep-down feeling right in your gut that *you* had better get organized. This is the way Willy organized the 1960 California Olympic races into the best-run winter games up to that time. Not only was it an Olympics for competitors, it was a *fun* Olympics.

Besides Kitz, there are several eastern Austrian resorts of interest. To the south are Zell am See, Saalbach, and Kaprun, all within easy post-dinner drive of each other. Smaller resorts abound.

Were this a travel guide, we could go into lifts and lengths, runs and elevations. They deserve— and have—books to themselves. To name the best of them: Foremost there is Abby Rand's *Ski Guide to Europe.* It is the only book that has pertinent room, board, and after-ski evaluations (not just listings) of some forty resorts, but unfortunately no terrain diagrams. *The Ski Runs of Austria* and *The Ski Runs of Switzerland,* both by James Riddell and published by Michael Joseph of London, are out-of-date but contain the only good drawings and descriptions of the more complex lift systems. After that, there is Egon Ronay's *Ski Europe,* published in London by the Automobile Association (of Great Britain). Ronay's listings are exhaustive but his evaluations minimal. It's a good handbook to give information on the smaller resorts. For the climbing skier, *Salute To the Skier: 100 Best Runs in Europe,* by Walter Pause (Harrap and Co., London), has descriptions and pictures "above the lifts."

Ski writers often find "new" resorts undiscovered by visitors—the prices are low, the clientele friendly, the lift lines nil, and the mountains magnificent. Kaprun fits this category. The Kitzsteinhorn glacier above Kaprun starts at the 10,000-foot top, an attractive, rolling, snow plain. By letting go, you get a technically demanding run, but basically the glacier's 3,000 vertical feet are very easy fun. Below are a tough 3,000 down to the valley. This is not always open, because the low altitude discourages good conditions. When it's skiable in its entirety, however, the Kitzsteinhorn run ranks with the most intriguing dozen lift-served descents in Europe.

The Kitzsteinhorn is impressive. The town is inexpensive. The Hotel Pension Orgler has prices in the $3 range, and food is not high. A six-day ticket and bed and board can come to something like $40. Kaprun is a relatively recent arrival as a major ski town. The glacier lifts are new, and there is no tourist weariness on the part of the townspeople. They seem bemused and helpful. The midwinter clientele is young, mostly students and quite likely to become enthusiastic over Americans or English in a student way.

Kaprun actually is not so far from the Italian Tyrol. It's easy to include Italy on a ski trip to Austria. Turn south at Innsbruck rather than going on toward the Arlberg Pass, go over the Brenner Pass and there you are. The number of English-speaking visitors skiing Italy has increased markedly, but tourism from the outside is still considerably less than outside traffic to eastern Austria and

Europe's terrain above the treeline confers magnificent gifts on expert and novice alike. Its varieties are enjoyed by redoubtable Sylvain Saudan at Courmayeur, Italy (opposite), and by tourists at Les Arcs and Tignes in the French Savoie (far l & above). Nowhere but in Europe are scooters a part of village life.

Switzerland. Eastern Italy had long been cut off by its barrier alps, the ruggedest in Europe, until better roads to and from the Brenner made the area more accessible.

Italy is not expensive, although the 1970's boom in Italy reduced the differences. Northern Italian food is a big, hearty plus. Italian after-ski ranks well above the French for robustness and jollity.

The Italians can be warmer than the Austrians or Swiss. Quite often there is no trouble joining Italians; if you are a reasonably proportioned woman, *au contraire*, the trouble is quite the opposite. The lean, wealthy look is everywhere. Clothes are smarter even than in St. Moritz. Italy has made it in the lineup of countries with a very well-to-do upper middle class, which has predictably taken exuberantly to conspicuous consumption.

Italy has two outstanding resorts in its eastern Dolomites. First is Val Gardena, a steep-sided valley of resorts with a half-dozen villages, whose available beds total 12,000, making Val Gardena as sizable as St. Moritz or Kitz. (Val Gardena is sometimes listed under Ortisei or Selva, the two best-known villages in the valley.) The valley was the site of· the 1970 World Championship and the skiing is great—everything from steep to slack, and lots of choices of type, exposure, and snow.

Cortina, the other eastern Italian resort, is a mountain capital, like Chamonix, and has the best after-ski in Italy, as good as any on the continent. Cortina's skiing is very good, with some of the steepest runs in the Alps.

Val and Cortina are about sixty miles —as the crow flies—over the Brenner Pass from Innsbruck. The actual drive can be up to a hundred miles. Flying into Munich and starting your skiing in Kitz, going over the Brenner to Cortina and Val, and then back to the Arlberg and over to Grisons makes a great three-week, three-country excursion.

The alternative way to ski Cortina and Val would be to fly to Milan and drive or bus three hundred miles from Milan. Train and plane transportation to the Dolomites has continued poor and erratic, so it's the road or nothing from Milan.

As a practical matter, you wouldn't go via Milan unless you love Italy more than most, speak Italian well, and want to ski nowhere but Italy. You can ski the Dolomites from Zurich and Munich, cities closer to a much greater variety of better skiing than Milan.

Back over the Brenner, now to go west again in Austria. The third busiest Austrian center of activity for visitors is in the Otztaler Alps down toward the Italian border at "the Gurgls." Obergurgl is a more cosmopolitan place than Kaprun (nearly always English-speaking guests around). There is lovely skiing in Obergurgl, the highest base-station in Austria. It claims to be the highest town-with-a-church in Austria. It lies at 6,300 feet and usually provides a superb snowpack. The roundabout towns are smallish, Hochgurgl very small, *à la* St. Christoph. Its skiing is high. From Hochgurgl you can ski glacier fields blithely until June. In mid-winter, if there is poor snow (as there can be in the eastern Alps), I would head toward "the Gurgls."

And so, over the Arlberg Pass to Switzerland. (We've already touched on the joys of St. Anton and the Arlberg.)

Europe's cafe life persists on high-mountain restaurants and sun porches. Here, at Chamrousse, site of the 1968 Winter Olympics outside Grenoble, skiers engage in gossip, greeting, girl-watching, and the gist of *Le Monde*.

Switzerland is in origin a collection of five counties or cantons of mountaineers who speak five different tongues and hold to five different sets of customs. The five cantons banded together because they could not stand belonging to anyone else, and today stand not so much united as a nation as pressed back to back to leave both hands free to handle money.

There is no such thing as a Swiss, then. There is the German Swiss in the east, the Italian Swiss to the south, and the French Swiss to the west. There is a Romanesque Swiss who speaks a form of Latin. Yet there *is* such a thing as a Swiss, certainly: polite, imperturbable, resourceful, impeccably honest, meticulous, smoothly opportunistic (you will not mind that—the Swiss does everything he says he will).

The Swiss resort is organized. A central committee in each village welds the hotel owners, lift operators, restaurateurs, shopkeepers, and bankers (who tend *de facto* to be among the chief planners) into a cohesive whole that produces a resort most competitive, clean, and coherent. There is no incoherence in Switzerland.

Ski photographer George Busch wrote, "I've got any number of friends who find this perfection depressing. No unemployment, no neglected minorities to fight for, no undeclared wars to demonstrate against, no penis envy, no gay revolution, no street gangs, no tear gas, no litter, no open classrooms—how the hell can you stir up a meaningful cocktail party conversation?"

Anybody traveling westward in Europe finds that prices go up as a concomitant of jumping from the Arlberg to eastern Switzerland. The language is the same (German), but you will be paying a good equivalent of American medium-high prices.

Let's take the most easterly group of Swiss resorts, just over the border from Austria. This is the Grisons group, consisting chiefly of St. Moritz, Davos-Par-senn, and Arosa. Once this was the group overwhelmingly patronized by Americans because of its proximity to the Arlberg. (In the early days, the Arlberg was where the Austrian instructor sent Americans.) The Grisons is only a short detour from the direct Wallen-Arlberg route. Instead of going through little Liechtenstein to Austria, you turn off at the end of the Walensee and go south to Landquart, about forty miles to arrive at Arosa, Davos, or Klosters. To go on to St. Moritz, you go south again some sixty miles from Landquart, and over a real uphill known as the Julien Pass.

On the occasion of my first trip to St. Moritz, I drove this route in a blizzard. As I got higher, the European drivers were backsliding and spinning all over the road. I had to stop and wait for a hole to appear in the sprawl of cars to start up each hill. Finally, near the top of the pass, the snow was too deep and the hill too steep. I was stymied and stopped at a gas station—the only gas station in the pass —and asked how much for a pair of chains (which the car rental company, bless its heart, had forgotten to put in the trunk). The man said forty dollars and I paid forty dollars, which was then a hell of a lot of money, even in Swiss francs. But it was a seller's market, and this was Switzerland.

Arosa was the first place in which I skied on European soil. That was a good many years ago, when the prop planes took seventeen hours to make it to Zurich. We went by train from Zurich right into Arosa, the end of the line. (Sometimes trains make sense.) A Swiss train is a marvel in and of itself. The upholstery, even in second class, is beautiful. In first class, luxurious. The food is better than you can find without protracted searching in the United States. The porters serve fruit and sandwiches. The windows are big picture windows, the views superb. It is clean, smooth-riding, up-to-date, on time, everything that the American railroads are not.

Arosa is an *old* Swiss resort, built under an imposing south-facing wall of snow with a 3,000-foot

The chase down the endless slopes of Europe is always fittingly set off with pleasant surroundings and garlanded with good food and drink. Typical is the *restaurant d'altitude* being appreciated by the author and his wife (center l) at Les Arcs. Above: Skiers airlifted to glacier begin descent.

vertical, all above treeline, roughly of a size equaled in snow acreage by Aspen-Aspen Highlands-Snowmass-Buttermilk. And no trees to tangle with.

When I arrived, Arosa's streets were covered with smooth-packed snow to let the horse sleighs do their work. They were the preferred transportation, even though special snow taxis could make the climbs. Arosa was clean, clean, clean. It made you feel laundered from head to toe just to stand there soaking in the cleanliness. The porter at the hotel took the bags, skis were whisked into the ski room, and retrieved instantly when I came back down. Where were all the skiers on the hill? Half the guests had come just to skate, sleigh, curl, and take walks. The lifts were never crowded. The sun shone all day. I had no trouble getting that exportable tan. Marvelous.

Besides lovely Arosa, the Grisons canton has the Davos-Parsenn, the world giant of skiing, whose size does not make it atypical of the huge multitown European ski complex, of which there are several. "The Parsenn," as the whole complex is called, dwarfs Zurs-Lech-St. Anton and is better integrated.

This utterly fantastic Parsenn terrain spreads over more snow than any other resort. To approximate the Parsenn, you would have to turn Mt. Washington and several neighboring Presidential peaks into a rampant commercial development, with about sixty trails wriggling down to six or seven towns on the valleys to both sides. The United States does not, and the world does not, have anything quite like the Parsenn.

The Parsenn massif is circumscribed by a valley circling to the west in which lie several villages including the large town of Davos, about 10,000 people, and the smaller ones, Küblis and Klosters. All are stops on the railroad from Landquart.

If you want to ski for ten miles running, you can do it off the top of the Weissfluhgipfel at the top of the Parsenn. It's a 6,000 vertical down to Küblis. This is where the famous Parsenn Derby downhill has been run every year since 1924. It's seven miles long and not too steep.

The next interesting Swiss ski group to the west is in the Bernese Oberland and is an example of a different kind of interconnection. *The* renowned towns of the Oberland--Mürren, Wengen, and Grindelwald—are skiable in one day from one room. You can leave Grindelwald by cog railway or lift and go to Kleine Scheidegg, the shoulder of the mighty Jungfrau, one of Switzerland's highest mountains. Here shift to the Jungfraubahn and go all the way—six miles—to the end, Jungfraujoch. There's a hotel overlooking all the glacier country; here they cut the famous Ice Palace out of the glacier for skating, and here you can ski tour (if you know your way around) all winter and summer. It's 11,000 feet up.

Wengen and Mürren below you are themselves perched on opposite rims of the deep-shadowed Lauterbrunnen valley. The only way to either Wengen or Mürren is by electric train or cable car from Lauterbrunnen; there are no roads. The result is two delightful, pre-internal-combustion-engine ski villages. Would there were more like them in the U.S. and elsewhere.

Returning on the Jungfraubahn, you can ski down the famous Lauberhorn trail to Wengen on the near side of the valley, and from Wengen you can take a train across to Mürren. A cable will take you to the top of the 10,000-foot Schilthorn. Ski back to Mürren, train to Wengen, up by cable to the Männlichen, and ski down to Grindelwald. It will be a long but exhilarating day.

The first modern slalom race was held at Mürren in January 1922, devised by Sir Arnold Lunn in his desire for more exciting and compact downhill competition. It was the first use of slalom poles, together with stopwatch timing to decide a ski race. There were many opposed to downhill in those days—mountain climbers who thought downhill racers were exhibitionists, and Scandinavians who wanted to keep skiing a sport confined to the pristine Nordic forms, cross-country and jumping.

"When God made the hills, he intended them to be climbed and not to be used as glorified toboggan runs," wrote a mountaineer in the *Alpine Journal*. Sir Arnold made a measured reply: "I was not consulted at the Creation and can therefore speak with no authority on the Intentions of the Creator. . . ."

A Scandinavian vice president of the International Ski Congress in St. Moritz asked Sir Arnold in 1928, "What would you think, Mr. Lunn, if we Norwegians tried to alter the rules of cricket?" Three years later, the traditionalists relented. The first world alpine ski championship was held at Mürren in 1931. Next to St. Anton, Mürren is the town most sacred to the history of skiing.

The final Swiss region of note is the Valais, plus the southwest Bernese Oberland going toward the French border. Here, naturally enough, the natives and the cuisine begin to veer toward the French.

During our westward trek, prices rise and hospitality tends to slide off a little, but paradoxically civility in the liftlines increases. The Germans and Austrians are a merciless mob in the liftlines. There is no liftline, in fact, only a disorderly crowd seeking to edge forward with sharpened elbows and crunching skis. By the time we reach the Valais, the crowd is only slightly more competitive and disorderly than those in the United States, a decided relief.

Of all the resorts in the west of Switzerland, Gstaad is the most edifying. It is the best-preserved "Old Swiss" in the country. The town is an assemblage of beautiful private chalets under the high towers of the Palace. (The Gstaad Palace is one of the three Palaces that count in skiing Switzerland.) The unique zoning of Gstaad keeps further large hotels from being built. So it is all very peasant-like, yet underneath the peasant roofs are some of the world's best-known, most elegant people. There is great skiing roundabout Gstaad.

For me, the most spectacular is at the Diablerets, some twenty miles off, where there's a tremendous run down the *jetes*, a series of big glacial cirques (like that at Tuckerman's Ravine in New Hampshire). They are carved out of mountain, I noted after my first descent, "as if by a god who had nothing better to do than idly scoop a number of immense depths out of white Carrara marble: glistening smooth, chillingly remorseless descents, a funnel down to infinity." Once you've run Diablerets, you've earned the right to go back to the Palace at tea time, go into the big, comfortably overfurnished sitting room, and order a small Napoleon. If charm is your object, Gstaad is your subject.

Zermatt, the most famous Valais resort, is a superb example of the transborder resort. It has a good deal of the best skiing in the Valais region, topped by descents from the 11,000-foot Stockhorn. You can also run past the Matterhorn and over the Theodul pass down to Cervinia, in Italy. This is one of Europe's most extraordinarily pleasant

Storm in Europe can be spectacular. Terrain is largely unprotected by tree cover and there are few landmarks to guide skiers through a blizzard. This is one reason Europeans employ more guides and instructors.

Scotland has spring skiing
in highland corries—these
valleys always fill with
deep snow. Skiers at largest
Scottish lift area,
Cairngorms (below & bottom),
ski content in the
corries all day and have
choice, good old-fashioned
Scottish resorts for
rest and recreation—as at
Grantown-on-Spey (r)
south of Inverness.

runs—down the Plateau Rosa, a five-mile stretch—it's one of those big 6,000-foot lift-served verticals in Europe. Hardly anybody stays a week in Zermatt without going over to Cervinia, and vice versa.

Zermatt is the third of the car-less Swiss villages; happily it can be reached only by cog railway. Its skiing alone has made Zermatt the busiest resort in western Switzerland. Not only are there the Zermatt skiers and Italians from the other side (who call the Matterhorn "Mt. Cervinia"), there are Haute Route skiers from the west coming down to this terminal of the route. Zermatt is a ski cosmos, the most varied ski center in Switzerland.

And so finally to France. There are gentle gradations of Swiss all across Switzerland to the French border. One canton melds with the next. But once you cross into France, there is an abrupt qualitative change in the people.

The French are less easy than the Swiss to join, to converse with, and to know. They appear to feel sufficient unto themselves, and only recently (and somewhat reluctantly) have they declared themselves in the competition for foreign ski trade. Having made the decision, the French went forward logically and directly. The result is the new high-rise "ships of the snow" that have been anchored in the Savoie. Whether the French have the right logic remains to be seen. There has been no rush of foreign skiers into these modern cities. But the achievement is immense.

Committed to building ski resorts with capacities exceeding their native skiing population, and faced with the necessity of making the new resorts popular with visitors, the French have had to become aware of public relations, however much this grates against the French character.

The slightly patrician French outlook extends most notably to the language. If you don't speak French well, the average French skier you meet—unless he is really taken with you—infinitely prefers that you not try at all. Conversely, the French feel that, in order to converse in English, they ought to be nearly grammar-perfect. Therefore they often will not try—even though they do have command of passable English. A stand-off.

The French are extremely gracious to those they accept. Theirs is not the surface acceptance of the American, which glosses over all differences for the sake of a casual short-run acquaintanceship, but a more arduous relationship.

Eh, bien. In Switzerland or Austria or Italy, nearly everywhere, the American is guaranteed a reasonably quick and reasonably superficial association with at least a few other non-English skiers. In France, where—except at Courchevel—the French normally comprise ninety percent of the skiers at any given resort, he is not so guaranteed. The American going to ski in France should take his own friends with him.

But the French professionals that the skier meets—waiters, maître d's, hotel managers, instructors—are the diplomats of the European ski world. The Austrians and Germans and Swiss may rub a bit the wrong way from time to time with rough country humor or by being insistently paternalistic; their French counterparts, never. The French have a developed instinct for psychological subtleties and a superb tradition in manners—when they want to use them—very soothing to the tired skier who comes down from a hard day on the hill.

The French have the most compact major ski zone in Europe. If you cut a rectangle 60 by 30 miles into the Alps just south of Geneva and the adjoining shore of Lac Léman, you have included *all* of the most interesting French skiing, both the old and new, in the Savoie and the Haute Savoie. To venture beyond the Savoie provinces will not give the skier any better skiing. The Swiss Valais and French Savoie, cheek by jowl, provide a western alpine region fully the equal to the eastern Alps' Arlberg-Davos-St. Moritz. A goodly group of expert skiers feels it surpasses all other regional groupings in the world.

The very peak of French skiing lies around Chamonix, the oldest, most conservative, least changed by time of all French ski towns. It's a medieval mountain capital, set in a deep dark gorge, with narrow cobbled streets and high hotels of a Victorian mien, built in the last century for the summer tourist trade. Chamonix has resonances of St. Moritz, but is more crowded and certainly as high-priced.

Chamonix is the outstanding example of the "scattered terrain resort." The combination of Chamonix's Grands Montets, Brévent, and the Mer de Glace adds up to the most formidable skiing gathered in one place in Europe, but "one place" extends for miles.

The Grands Montets is a steep, north-facing, wide-open slope several miles out of town. It starts down from 10,800 feet on a glacier over the valley. For sheer fun and carefree speed, the Grands Montets is surely among the best slopes in Europe.

The Brévent, also outside town, is shorter, steeper, and narrower; because it faces east you get an absolutely staggering panorama on a clear day: the dome of Mt. Blanc, the sharp needle rocks (les Aiguilles), and the wall of the Jorasses, and the glaciers descending in ponderous sweeps to the black forests on the other side. The top part is probably the most demanding lift skiing in the Alps.

Spring is the time of the Mer de Glace (in Abby Rand's book—by a typographical error—it's called "Merde Glace"). The Aiguille du Midi cable car, the highest in the Alps (to 11,500), takes you to the top of the run and the restaurants where you can look down to see if you can catch the glacier moving as you finish your preparatory meal. This is basically a glacier run, and the only difficulty is to know the right snowbridges. The skiing is easy. It goes and goes and goes—ten miles. You need a guide.

In late spring, you can also go by cable from l'Aiguille over the Vallée Blanche by the Dent du Géant and down the Italian side of the Mt. Blanc massif to Entrèves, a taxi ride away from the resort village of Courmayeur. Or, anytime in the season, you can drive through the ten-mile Mt. Blanc tunnel, from Chamonix to Courmayeur, an eerie ride deep in a mine shaft. It may be sunny on the Courmayeur side when the weather is gray in Chamonix, so the tunnel is a great resource for Chamonix skiers.

An intriguing place, Chamonix, but don't get stuck here without a car; Chamonix is hard to ski from. All the major base stations are outside of town, and the bus system is fitful—to be kind.

The famed resort of Val d'Isère, where the triple Olympic medalist Jean-Claude Killy comes from, has the best odds for good skiing. Val's toughest terrain is not so extreme as at Chamonix, but it's pretty tough. Val, alone of the old French resorts, is set above the treeline, at 6,000 feet. (Chamonix is at 3,000.) The top of Val is about 10,000, and you can get there quickly. The terrain has the best snow record in the eastern Alps.

Val as a town is a conglomerate of bad old architecture and bad new architecture, and has not much charm except for the skier who likes to ski. For him, Val has all kinds of charm. It is an American's ski town. Generally Americans like skiing more than after-skiing and while Val is not much for night life it does give you the most powder snow. If you like snow, you'll like Val. European powder, generally, is not normally as prevalent, dry, or reliable as the powder in Utah, or even in the Rockies. This accounts for European skiers' enthusiastic visits to the West. The U.S. can't show Europeans much in terrain, but it sure can show them powder snow. But at Val the snow is dry.

Val is popular with the French themselves. On the slope, the French generally are the fastest, brashest, and least considerate skiers in Europe. They nearly all ski parallel turns of a sort, thanks to the Allais influence on the ski-teaching method. But it's a slewing kind of turn that allows the skier, if he's so inclined, to go much too fast for his ability. And few French skiers stop and say *Pardon* if they carom off another skier. They keep going. *Tant pis.* Too bad. You were in the way.

The most popular French resort among Americans is Courchevel. This was built after the old resorts but before the new ones. It is not quite the monolith that the newest are, but it is built well up into reliable snow line, with a very well integrated lift system, smooth slopes constantly groomed, acres and acres and acres of intermediate terrain—the Vail of Europe.

There are two ways to more demanding adventure in Courchevel. The first is via Air Alps airport. Air Alps will take you to one of several outstanding nearby glacier runs in a STOL plane (short-takeoff-and-landing) equipped with skis. Air Alps knows which glacier is ripe for skiing today. The glaciers round about are normally very benign and the runs long and exhilarating, but not steep. The fascinating thing about glaciers is the way the "terrain" changes. The runs are sculptured by mountain winds out of pure snow.

The second way to adventure is to "ski the Trois Vallées": Over the top at Courchevel, down to Méribel, and up again over the next ridge to Les Menuires. It's one day out and one day back, if you go in a crazy hurry. Otherwise, it makes a nice, peripatetic week without having to get into a car. Bea and I skied the Trois Vallées a few years ago with another American couple. Skiing down to Méribel turned out to be a bit of an exercise in rough snow. We found that the French down-unweighting technique, which works so smoothly on the groomed slopes we'd left behind, was not really applicable to the ungroomed snow, which calls for up-unweighting and getting the skis turned in the air a bit. But we made it down. Méribel is as rustic and old-fashioned a little ski village as exists in France. Charming. Then we got

to Les Menuires and we were in the most modern of the new French high-rise resorts.

Our host at the Hotel Skilt in Les Menuires served us a simple little welcome: a three-course late lunch, with wine; he opened the glass doors of the dining room so we were in effect outdoors but protected from the breeze. The sun streamed in, and the wine streamed down, and we stretched our legs. *La belle France!*

And a third shot at Italy makes sense while you are in the Savoie: Courmayeur, a painless thirty-minute drive from France through the Mt. Blanc tunnel. The attractions of Courmayeur are that you can get there in any weather from Chamonix, that it's a largish, nice-looking mountain town without too much of a touristy air about it. It has a couple of great restaurants: Maison de Filippo and La Brenva. The skiing is okay but grooming is rudimentary; when you take their "long run" from Cresta d'Arp, seven miles down the spectacular Youla valley to Dolonne, the first stop on the Courmayeur gondola, you will have exercised everything you know about rough-snow skiing unless conditions are unusually friendly.

At Courmayeur I had my only actual brush with a live avalanche. Bea and I had ascended with photographer Del Mulkey to Cresta d'Arp to shoot pictures of Sylvain Saudan, the Swiss steep-descent specialist whose courage is hair-raising. We had been told that the run from the top down the Youla valley to the drag lift (the way to the seven-mile run to Dolonne) was open. A track down the slope from the glass-enclosed restaurant at Cresta d'Arp had been machine-packed, but we traversed to the wall at the head of the valley to get out to the steep skiing, where Saudan could do his stuff for the camera. Suddenly, two-thirds of the wall in front of us shook, blurred, and started moving like a giant rug being pulled down into the valley. We kick-turned rapidly and walked carefully back on our track while the avalanche —growing to huge proportions—rumbled and bounced down into the floor of the Youla and sailed a good hundred feet up the other side.

It was a wet-snow avalanche, an Amazon river of big and little snowballs. None of us would have survived it had we been on the wall when it started. Once again: In Europe, "open" means "open where tracked," not "open everywhere."

Saudan was not disturbed and insisted that we take his picture with the avalanche still running in the background. After the rest of us caught our breath and restored our courage, we skied down the machine-packed trail into the section crossed by the avalanche and tried skiing over the humped snowballs of avalanche snow, an enterprise at which only Saudan was particularly successful, as can be seen in the picture on page 110.

After a day of shooting, we trekked to Maison de Filippo and ate ourselves into a stupor in Italian, five enormous courses ending with a café alle Valdostana. This is to ordinary coffee as Mt. Blanc is to a golf tee, a blend of coffee, fruit, and enough grappa so it can be served flaming. By the time we'd finished the hot bowl (the waiters cheering us on), we'd forgotten that we had almost ended the day on that great ski hill in the sky. *Arrivederci, Italia.*

What is now left on the continent?

There are Greece and Yugoslavia, of course. Mt. Olympus and the Julian Alps are skied by a few. There are the Czech Carpathians and the Caucasus. But all this is strictly exotic skiing.

Somewhat more mundane yet frequently delightful are the remaining resorts of the west. For one, there is the skiing "du Midi," south of the Savoie. After you fly to Grenoble, it's not so hard to get either to Alpe d'Huez or Deux Alpes, both very nice resorts. When the Savoie has bad snow, the Midi can have beautiful snow.

Across the Alps from Grenoble there's Italy's Sestriere, the fifth of the five top Italian resorts.

Sestriere is the first premeditated ski resort in the world, originally envisioned by the Fiat company in 1931 as two round, silo-like hotels with circling ramps inside (instead of stairs, like the Guggenheim Museum in New York). Sestriere is high, nearly 7,000 feet at the base. Snow is good and so is the skiing. It's a big resort with seventy runs and 2,700 vertical. But again you have roughly two hundred rugged miles from either Milan or Geneva. Via Grenoble is best.

Here it is apropos to consider the auto passes of the Alps. On the map it looks as if the drive from the French Midi over the Col du Montgenèvre into Sestriere, forty miles off, might be feasible. And so it might. In fact, it's open most of the time. And it's quicker from Geneva than going through the Mt. Blanc tunnel. But, nearly every pass—from the Arlberg and Brenner in the east to Montgenèvre in the west—has its own weather.

In a high alpine track you may get snow while the village in the plain below has sun or showers. So it is in the passes. It takes only a couple of inches of slippery snow and a couple of inexperienced drivers to block or choke a pass. The roads themselves are often hazardous enough in clear, dry weather. In a snow storm, with limited visibility, the passes can be lethal.

It's often difficult—if not impossible—to get accurate information on conditions in the passes. Montgenèvre is right in the pass, so you can call there, but it becomes clear, on the whole, that the idea of going by way of the passes —except the Arlberg and Brenner, which are on main arteries— is like rolling dice. This is especially true in the western Alps. Avoriaz and Gstaad south of Lac Léman are only about thirty miles apart over the ridge of the Alps as *le corbin* flies. But it's a much better idea to plan to drive a hundred and some miles through Geneva, going north of Lac Léman on the relatively low-altitude divided highway, than to go direct.

Closer to the sun than the Midi are the Pyrenees. The Pyrenees roads are miserable, but Super-

differently the world looks to Norwegians.

Norway is a fine place for British and Americans who like touring. The average high-school graduate has had from five to seven years of English and is delighted to practice it. The instructors, over the years, have worked out subtle ways of imparting the spirit and substance of touring to pupils.

One could even stay right in Oslo—a relatively warm, absolutely clean, cosmopolitan place with superb restaurants and museums—and go by rail every day out to the last stop, which is Nordmarka. The skis go into racks on the outside of the cars.

After Nordmarka, get on the Oslo-Bergen railroad and make for Finse in the middle, the country's most renowned touring center. Finse itself is small—a few hotels and inns—but it lies at the edge of Hardangervidda, a hundred-mile stretch of touring country marked by lines of cut saplings to show where the course lies.

A *vidda* is the typical, widely prevalent terrain in central Norway: a plateau lying at about 3,000 feet which consists of wide-open, gently undulating country, polished by many centuries of severe glacial abrasion. The vidda gives the emotional impact of great space, like the American plains. There is enough variation to avoid monotony, a few steep valleys, a few high peaks. Norwegians ski without guides, using compass and map to navigate this rolling ocean of the mountains. Hardangervidda thus bred in men the secure belief that a pair of skis could take them anywhere in the country. And did. The long Viking ski has more than aesthetics in common with the Viking ship.

One of my own most memorable ski weeks consisted of hiking some forty miles through the Hardangervidda with Kim Massie and Mike Brady, an American engineer living in Oslo, who supplied a brace of photogenic Oslo girls in their late teens, each of whom could outski me by about fifty percent on an average five-hour trek.

Touring technique is easy to learn at the beginning, hard to perfect. You have to be fast and go for miles. It's like learning the stride of the long-distance runner. You have to acquire a view of the body as an instrument to be brought to a well-tempered whole, capable of grace under endurance conditions. The Norwegians believe that this state of mind and body leads to clear thinking.

In the Hardangervidda, the hotels and inns lie scattered at appropriate five- or six-hour intervals on the marked tracks, standing alone like offshore buoys in the swells of snow, sustaining way-stations. These inns have the famous smörgasbord—cured and salted meats, cheese and delicately smoked salmon, marinated fish, sourdough breads, as well as warm dishes—country cooking of an extraordinarily welcome sort.

The daily routine: Get out of bunk bed, dress, breakfast at the inn, wax skis, secure lunch packs, and set out. The wide rolling hills of the vidda are deserted, or nearly so. The track goes straight on under the sky. You move into your stride, settle there, and soon are almost detached, a pilot of your body, sensing it as the captain senses the motion of his ship—a peaceful remoteness. Occasionally you ski two by two and talk.

The lunch break: smoked salmon and cured meat and a draught of mountain water. Onward. The fourth hour your detachment begins to fade under a wave of fatigue. The fifth hour is one of hanging in there until the last thirty minutes, when a mysterious surge of power quickens your arms and legs because there is the inn on the far side of the smooth valley. Only thirty minutes more and you can have a long draught of Export beer and collapse companionably until the spirit rallies with the appearance of the first plates of the fragrant evening meal. A roomful of hardy tour skiers starts moving, with long touring strides, to well-laden tables. The thought may hit you just then, that this has been one of your perfect days.

A sentinel peak on the Atlantic Coast, Mt. Agamenticus in Maine, is the first lift area in the United States to see the morning sun. Four thousand miles to the west, at Alyeska in Alaska, the sun finally sets on the last American ski resort. Between these two are some 1,500 ski areas of all shapes and sizes, with a total of more than 5,000 lifts, scattered through forty-four of the Union's fifty states and in nine Canadian provinces. (Mexico has skiing but no lifts.) America has more lifts than Europe by a considerable margin.

To make a more relevant comparison, however, first define an American heartland of skiing similar to Europe's, that is, containing ninety percent of the continent's best skiing. From the eastern slope of the Rockies, at Denver, go due west on the 40th parallel across Colorado, across Utah, across Nevada. Keep on going across Lake Tahoe, at the California border, and stop on the western slope of the Sierra Nevada. This establishes an 800-mile east-west dimension. The 35th parallel south of this line and the 45th north of it (each about 350 miles away) serve as top and bottom boundaries. Inside are Alta, Snowbird, and Park City in Utah; Aspen, Vail, and Snowmass in Colorado; Squaw Valley, Heavenly Valley, Sugar Bowl, and Mammoth in California; Jackson Hole in Wyoming; Sun Valley in Idaho; Taos in New Mexico— in all, ninety percent of the best. The rectangle is eight times as large in area (560,000 sq. mi.) as that needed to enclose Europe's heartland (70,000 sq. mi.). That is what is meant by the compactness of European skiing. Europe has other formidable advantages.

The phrase "ski area" means nothing more than the presence of lifts. Go beyond that definition, and say that a "resort" is a ski area within commuting distance of five hundred beds available for rent; then Europe's heartland has something like three hundred resorts, while America's has fewer than a hundred.

Define an even more exclusive category. Call it "destination resorts." Set the minimum at a thousand beds within commuting distance and say that the resort has to draw at least half of its skiers from outside the country, or from at least a day's drive away, and that at least a third stay overnight. Finally, say that the resort has to have terrain so extensive and varied that a good skier could enjoy skiing it for a week. On that basis, the European heartland has at least seventy destination resorts, the American heartland less than a dozen. Further, European destination resorts occasionally occur in clusters of five or more within a radius of fifty air miles. This happens in Savoie, Haute Savoie, Valais, the Bernese Oberland, the Grisons, and the Arlberg. The best the American heartland can boast is three triplets of clustered destination resorts, no quadruplets, no quintuplets.

A third means of comparison: Define a ski city as having the size and dedication to skiing of a Val d'Isère. Then Europe's heartland has about twenty such, the American—at most—has eight.

Finally, the European heartland has longer trails, greater verticals, and more civilized après-ski. This raises the question: Is there any way in which American skiing is better? The answer is yes. Resort density, slope vertical, and après-ski sophistication are not the only measures of a first-rate ski country. The most important factors are the actual conditions on the slope where the skiing takes place.

First, the American resorts have more snow than any broad region of Europe. The Sierra and Wasatch ranges get better than 450 inches total snowfall a winter, which works out to 37 feet, 6 inches before it's packed down. Colorado gets an average of 20 feet. There is more snow in Colorado's main skiing zone (between 8,000 and 10,000 feet) than in the main European zone (between 6,000 and 8,000 feet). In Europe the snow is normally not reliable at 6,000 feet until mid-December, by which time the skiers in Colorado have been skiing for two or three weeks.

Because the Rockies and the Wasatch are insulated from the oceans by dry continental basins, their

snow is drier, more consistent, and more resilient than Europe's—and there is no *föhn*, or south wind, off the Mediterranean to turn good snow into less tractable boilerplate.

Icy boilerplate is rare in the West. On an average western ski day, hard-packed, even slightly icy base protrudes here and there, but the two to five inches on top, where the quality of the ride is determined, will be softer, springier, and more exhilarating than Europe's average snow.

Weather, of course, creates comfortable—or uncomfortable skiing. Ideally, temperatures should not jump around so that the skier is sweating one day and frozen the next. An even, cool temperature is best for both skier and snow. The West has relatively stable, predictably cool skiing above 7,000 feet, a weather rather magnificently regulated for skier and snow. There is little winter rain of consequence, seldom a winter thaw of much penetration, or a long, sub-zero cold spell. There are cold spots in the Rockies, but few have been turned into ski resorts.

For consistently good snow and good skiing, slopes must have an exposure and forest cover offering protection from the prevailing strong winds. The magnificent, above-treeline skiing of Europe is glorious as long as the wind and snow do not blow. When they do—and it happens often enough—the European skier has problems of comfort, visibility, and navigation. The treeline in Europe's central alpine massif is at about 6,000 feet, far below the best-quality snow.

Protection in the American West is superb. The treeline in Colorado, for instance, reaches 11,500 feet. Generally, the open slopes of the West consist of man-made or natural glades surrounded by woods. There is ample protection for skiing at the best altitudes, provided the trail design is thoughtful.

Tree protection makes it possible to ski in comfort and serenity in stronger winds and, just as crucially, it encourages falling snow to settle in an even, feathery blanket which is preferable to having wind drive the snow into drifts and create less desirable forms, such as slab, wind crust, and wind pack.

Another concern is slope accessibility. The valleys of Europe, to generalize again, are deep and dark. They go down to within a few thousand feet of sea level. Thus, going up to the best skiing, above 7,000 feet, can involve an hour or more on cable cars and lifts.

The European alternative to having the village in the valley is having the village on the mountain, as the French have done in the new Savoie resorts. But this requires enormous investment, massive structures, and leads to a "new city" kind of feeling that is not necessarily as marketable as the *gemütlich* old-mountain-village look. The economic success of the "ships of the Alps" is still in the process of being proved.

The valleys of the American high mountains are high, wide, and sunny, offering ideal conditions for easy resort development (as well as the temptation to over-develop). American villages are much higher than Europe's. The large resorts of Colorado and Utah are all above 8,000 feet at the village level; there are no ski villages in Europe above 8,000. In the Sierra, the large resorts are in valleys at least 6,000 feet high. In Europe only a few villages are at 6,000 or above—Tignes, Courchevel, La Plagne, Val d'Isère, Cervinia, Hochgurgl, Val Gardena, and Sestriere notably.

In the American West it's a quick ride to the best skiing, and at the end of the day the skier can ski back to the village on good snow. In the course of a vacation week this is an undisguised blessing.

A final concern is the character of the terrain. No matter how good a skier is, he will not enjoy skiing very steep terrain all day long. Even a good skier needs a leavening of rolling, gently sloping terrain, and the average skier needs a lot of it in order to enjoy a ski week.

The contour of the American high mountains is more benign than Europe's. Mountain meadows

Opening pages: Powder
is the promise of America.
It happens best in the
West. Here snow falls dry
and fluffy from the Denver
face of the Rockies to the
Salt Lake slope of the Wasatch.
The West has the best snow
conditions in the world.

Skiing in the Appalachian
East: Rime on the trees,
village church steeples,
snow-making machines misting
across the trail in early
morning to soften the
surface. At Stratton, Vermont
(opposite), machines are
capable of covering trails
from midpoint on mountain
down to the base—just
the stretch where the legendary
eastern bunny needs help.

mix with the steeper terrain, from the top of the resorts to the bottom. There's nearly always an easy way around or down, one that's obvious, enjoyable, and well cared for, and this is not true nearly so often in Europe.

To sum up, the skier in western America is in a favored land. He's skiing a perfect world of fine, dry snow, in a relatively cool, stable climate, insulated from wind, rolling through medium-gradient snowfields that are free of ruts, bumps, and rocks. He gets to and from this lovely skiing quickly. Such a skier is not overly concerned about the extra thousand or so of vertical he might have had if he'd been skiing in Europe. Nor does he worry that there aren't five other resorts within a five-hour drive, or that the inn where he is staying is not up to *haute cuisine*. He's happy.

American high-mountain ski country offers the best guarantee anywhere of an A-1 skiing experience. The West is America's pride. It's a paradox, then, that most American skiers will never ski the West. The greater part of the American ski experience occurs outside its heartland, outside the high-mountain country altogether, to a considerable extent below 3,000 feet above sea level. In this respect American skiing is different from all other alpine-oriented countries, except Japan.

The East's Appalachian terrain, to begin with that, is a long way from the heartland. It is a ski anomaly running the length of the Appalachian Trail. This famous footpath works its way north from Spring Mountain, Georgia, through Chattahoochee country, through the Great Smoky Mountains of the Carolinas, across the Mason-Dixon Line into Delaware, up the Hudson River Valley to the Adirondacks of New York, east to the Green Mountains of Vermont, the White Mountains of New Hampshire, and the Blue Mountains of Maine. Here, on top of Mt. Katahdin, 2,015 miles from the start, the Appalachian Trail ends. Within a day's drive of the Trail live 125 million Americans, more than half the population of the United States. If the Canadian re-sorts along the Laurentian scarp are included, the East has more than five hundred lift areas.

The anomaly is that the skiing in these mountains lies below an altitude at which the good skiing in the West and Europe begins. Appalachian peaks rarely top 5,000 feet. Only Mt. Washington in New Hampshire and Mt. Mitchell in North Carolina top 6,000. Appalachian resort skiing is centered between 2,000 and 3,000 feet.

The exception to this is in western North Carolina, along the Tennessee border in the Great Smokies, where several resorts cluster at 5,000 feet. Beech Mountain goes to 5,400, with a gondola and five chairlifts. Cataloochee goes to 5,400 and Sugar Mountain to 5,300. These are the only eastern lifts over 5,000. The North Carolina cluster forms the center of the "bananabelt" of skiing, the southern segment of the Appalachians including Sky Valley, Georgia, about eighty miles north of Atlanta, and Cloudmont, near Mentone, Alabama; these are the two southernmost ski areas of the East. Aided by the altitude and snow-making machines, the Old Confederacy manages to keep some twenty viable ski resorts going all winter.

Ninety-five percent of Appalachian skiing is done north of the Mason-Dixon Line, and ninety percent of that below 4,000 feet. Only two northern resorts have lifts going over 4,000 feet: Cannon in New Hampshire and Whiteface in New York. This makes the Appalachians lower as a whole than any chain of popular ski mountains in the world, except Norway's Hardangervidda and the Scottish Highlands. Thus, Appalachian skiers all ski what is, predictably, the world's most unpredictable skiing. A rain will ruin five to twenty inches of snow cover overnight. And then it gets cold. The trails' slush turns to sheet ice. Not smooth sheet ice. Bumpy sheet ice. But because the majority of large eastern cities are no more than a day's drive from skiing in the Appalachians and Laurentians, the greater number of the 4.5 million Americans who ski spend the greater part of their time in these two areas.

Here they disburse the greater part of the $1.5 billion spent on the sport by Americans. This makes the eastern seaboard the biggest single regional ski economy in the world.

Nowhere have so many skied over such high-tensile snow for so long a time as in the East. The history of uphill transport had its beginning here. The first rope tow was put up in 1932 on Fosters Hill in Shawbridge, Quebec. Within two years several more pioneer tows were erected, one at Belknap, near Laconia, New Hampshire, and a second, more famous rope at Gilberts Hill, a sheep pasture in Woodstock, Vermont. A rope at Suicide Six, down the road from Gilberts, was soon strung over an honest-to-goodness twenty-degree pitch. Downhill skiing was underway.

The East has developed a good round dozen winter resort towns, notably Stowe, Waitsfield, Wilmington, Manchester, Franconia, North Conway, Hunter, St. Sauveur, and Lake Placid. And the ski resorts themselves, separate from the towns, are sizable, demographically if not topographically. For instance, Killington, in an area no more than a quarter that of Vail, produces, next to Vail, the largest annual gross receipts of any resort in the country: more than $6 million.

The neighboring American ski arena is the Midwest, a region without a serious mountain to call its own. The resorts cluster on the shores of the Great Lakes. There are one hundred and fifty ski areas in Minnesota, Michigan, Wisconsin, and Illinois. From these states, skiing spreads thinly in all directions. At the turn of the 1970's Iowa had nine ski areas, Missouri two, Kansas one, Arkansas one, Nebraska one, and South Dakota one.

The Midwest ski population outnumbers that in the West and on the Pacific Coast simply by virtue of hordes of skiers—from cities like Chicago, Milwaukee, Detroit, Minneapolis, St. Paul. They ski on small hills—no, sometimes mounds—and lots of snow driven in off the Lakes. The world can be searched for another lowland of skiing that is visible at 500 feet above sea level. None will be found.

The Midwest is particularly interesting because it brings the American skier's typical qualities to an extreme pitch. Since the Midwest offers little challenging terrain, the skier's interest centers on technique. This fascination with technique separates Americans from Europeans generally. An American skier can be perfectly happy working on his technique; he is willing to undertake a mechanistic appreciation of skiing. This produces a technically proficient trail skier very quickly.

The traditional European approach, in contrast, is the Germanic "nature appreciation" approach. The goal of the pioneer teacher, Zdarsky, was to get people down safely after having had the glorious climb up amid the "winter wonders of nature." The European skier is thus not distressed at having sunk into a life of stem turns. His highest moments come in attaining some choice vista during a particularly successful *itinéraire*, which only incidentally provides a downhill run. The highest moments of an American skier come in successfully connecting a few parallel turns, or some other definitive technical triumph, regardless of the place, the time, and the kind of hill on which he happens to be.

On snow, an American appreciates a consistency of texture and slope, rather than vagaries. The American resort has obliged with superhighways of skiing—wide, easy, smooth. Mt. Snow was the first eastern "superhighway" resort. Its success—stunning in comparison to older resorts like Stowe and Mad River, which had rough, European-style terrain—made Mt. Snow widely copied, right down to the 1970's French resorts in Savoie. Even the western skier likes his superhighway, as can be seen in the enormous success of Vail.

There is no shame in all this. Fanatics who bolt down steep faces in deep powder, or who bash over tough moguls, represent a level of dexterity won only by a couple of seasons of forty to fifty days' skiing. Most American

Sinuous, exciting trails of
East are cut through heavy
timber. Opposite: Green
Mountains of Vermont roll to
horizon in front of skier
on Glen Ellen's Rim Run.
Jay Peak's cable car
(far l) is East's most modern
uphill conveyance. East
often has good snow, but at
popular resorts like Bromley
(above) and Magic Mt. (l),
trick is to get to it fast.

skiers get no more than ten days, let alone fifty, a year. The Texans who leave the dry winter plains to divert themselves in Colorado prefer—much prefer—trails that allow a certain amount of high-speed machismo, without having to subject themselves for hours and hours to ski teachers. So do most American skiers, in fact.

On their wide, smooth, meticulously maintained trails, American intermediates of no more than twenty days' experience become reasonably skillful parallel skiers. This wide base of fairly good skiers makes the American ski population the most technically proficient in the world. Europeans of similar experience probably do no better than a simple stem turn. (The American, in fairness, however, is usually awful in rough snow where the British or Austrian stem plugger has a more stable approach.)

There has been in the past decade a gathering reaction against the American emphasis on a technical progress. It has taken the form of enormously increased interest in tour skiing, where technique is initially less demanding. The ratio of fifteen or twenty alpine skiers to one tour skier will hold in the U.S. this decade, but the balance is swinging. Nearly every downhill resort today has touring trails plus an instructor or two versed in touring, and often an overnight cabin, or at least a shelter, to serve as a windbreak for a trail lunch. For the first time American instructors in some number have learned how to teach touring. Teaching methods have been elaborated and a number of technical touring books are available, including this writer's *The Pleasures of Cross Country Skiing*.

While defections to touring continue, alpine skiing in America continues to burgeon. New skiers replace the annual drop-out rate of about twenty percent (due to early discouragement, arrival of children, old age, or accident). They increase the total something like ten percent per year, despite soaring prices for equipment and lift tickets, overcrowded roads, and the disappearance of most low-cost lodging.

Inscribing composite patterns in virgin snow is one of skiing's more recherché pleasures. Here, on a steep face at Jackson Hole, Wyoming, the surface has been decorated with near-military precision, amid some of the West's steepest and best skiing.

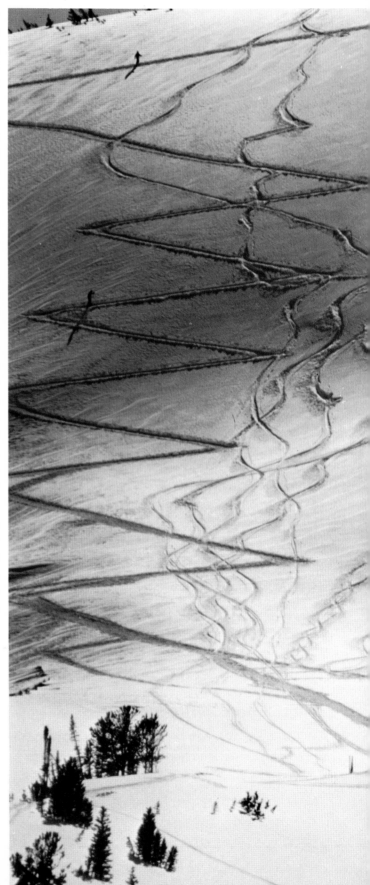

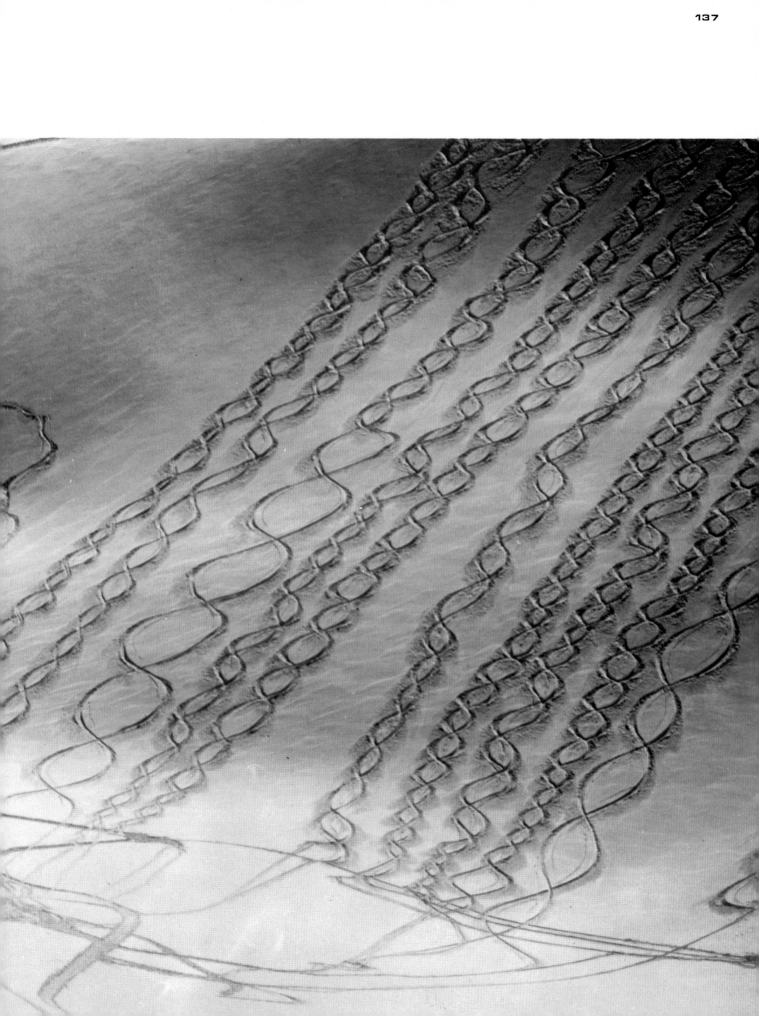

Flatlands of skiing run
1,300 miles, from Pittsburgh to
Denver: Meccas are Boyne Mountain,
Michigan (opposite), and Playboy
Club at Lake Geneva, Wisconsin
(above). Snow guns keep
skiing alive in South, where
Beech Mountain, North Carolina
(center), is biggest resort.

Twenty years ago things were simpler. I cite three Bowdoin College skiers—I was one—who liberated a jumbo jar of peanut butter and four loaves of bread from the fraternity kitchen, got a free tank of gas from one set of parents, and with less than $50 among them drove north to Lac Beauport, Quebec, then to Stowe, and back to Brunswick, Maine. The trip took five days, three of which were spent skiing at $3 per lift ticket per day. The remaining $23 went for gas and luxuries. Today one of these undergraduates is a partner of a firm on Wall Street. He and his wife take a week at Vail every winter, flying both ways, staying at a good inn there. They consider the $1,000 it costs well spent.

Some of the increase in the lift-ticket price in the East and Midwest comes from the costs of snow-making. A snow-making machine simply reproduces the physical conditions under which snow occurs naturally. There are two feed-ins to a snow-making nozzle. Compressed air is shot from one at a stream of water coming from the second. The expansion of the air cools the water and, at the same time, breaks it into droplets that freeze as snow particles. Man-made snow is not beautiful powder. It's wet and heavy. But it lasts and it's infinitely better than blue ice, green ice, or boilerplate, the natural conditions it replaces.

For skiers, snow-making's biggest drawback—besides expense—is that its flakes spew horizontally across the trail. This is all right at night or in early morning, but occasionally management will turn on the nozzles during skiing hours to try to keep the trails from going to sheer ice. If you wear glasses, the snow machine will coat them white, like an arctic freighter's rigging, and your sweater will be covered with hoarfrost. But it's better than skiing ice.

Snow-making has been imported to the West. Keystone, just over Loveland Pass in Colorado, put in top-to-bottom snow-making in the early 1970's, after the resort polled its skiers on what they wanted most and got the answer, "Better snow conditions." Other western resorts followed.

But it is in the East and Midwest that the real impact has been felt. The season has been extended. Christmas used to be the kick-off day. Now it's Thanksgiving. That difference represents a fifth of the potential revenue for the season.

Eastern ice is not simply the result of wet snow and low temperatures. It is created by putting snow under pressure, by compaction from the weight of many skis. The only way to save a busy eastern run from going to ice almost immediately is either snow-making or ice-breaking. Resort operators have created ice-fighting machines that comb the slopes, crunch the surface ice, grind it up, and spit it out again as skiable particles.

The other concomitant of heavy traffic is moguls. A series of "mogul choppers" has been invented to keep the ubiquitous mounds from growing to monster size. The mogul-fighting machines necessarily operate on some of the steeper slopes and require hardy drivers. All "cat" drivers know of machines that have rolled, if they haven't rolled one themselves. It's not much fun to toboggan a $10,000 machine upside down into the trees. But the skiing must go on. So the mogul-choppers and ice-fighters grind up and down the slopes, and the snow nozzles roar, and the skiers ski on trails that are smooth and accommodating far beyond the ken of your old-

time eastern or European skiers.

America not only has artificially prepared trails and artificially made snow, it also has artificial hills. These have been pioneered—naturally enough—in the Midwest, where there's a dearth of even small hills. One of the early hill-builders was John Blintz, an apple grower near Saginaw, Michigan. In the process of building himself an irrigation reservoir next to his orchards, Blintz decided he'd turn the excavated dirt into a ski mountain and put a lift on it. The first Apple Mountain was sixty feet high and so popular that Blintz kept on heaping it with dirt. Today it has a respectable two-hundred-foot vertical, eight lifts, eight snow-making nozzles, a ski shop, a ski school, and a day lodge. A second hill is being piled up not far away.

Even more promising man-made hills are being made of processed sanitation fill. One wit, seeing such a mountain of convenience, called it "Mt. Trashmore." Waste disposal is a growing municipal problem, so the country is being dotted with Mt. Trashmores. The techniques for mixing trash and garbage with earth, and keeping the drainage from running off harmfully at the bottom, have been worked out, solving ecological and recreational problems in one sophisticated stroke of recycling. These artificial hills, naturally, are being built close to the market, the city. Such near-city ski areas offer immediate opportunities for expanding American skiing.

Practically speaking, there is an inordinate number of city dwellers who will never be able to pay the costs involved in overnight trips to more distant slopes. The close-city resort cuts out all the frills. Get out there in the morning, get on the skis, and go back home at night. Total cost will be equipment rental (or depreciation) plus lift ticket plus transportation plus lunch.

Large eastern cities are being ringed with mini-hills, from micro- to macro-mini. One of the more enterprising macro-mini resorts in the New York City area is Great Gorge, some fifty miles from Times Square, across the George Washington Bridge, in McAfee, New Jersey. With a nearly 1,500-foot vertical, this is one of the largest resorts in the country in terms of ski population. There is a vast acreage under the guns of snow machines, a fleet of snow-grooming vehicles, plus an adjoining Playboy Hotel, and as much business as the place can handle.

On the other end of the scale is a micro-mini called Missionary Mountain, subsidized by the New York Missionary Society for Harlem youngsters. This is an example of an on-going socialization of skiing, but the sport doesn't yet qualify as the most democratic in the U.S. It's a sport in which a limited number of people spend a lot of money, more than is spent by twice as many people on golf, for instance.

There are all kinds of questions, sociological and ecological, about the soundness of increasingly intensive use of big mountains for resorts. Americans are debating the questions with much more earnestness than Europeans. The upshot is that the birthrate of big resorts has been dropping.

The American hills nevertheless are still less crowded in the current decade than they were twenty or thirty years ago, simply because the number of lifts has kept ahead of the number of skiers. Not once in the past ten years have I ever had to wait in line for as long as an hour. During my college ski weekends such a wait was not unusual. The longest lift lines at Aspen occurred in the 1950's when there was only a single chair going up a single mountain in the morning. Today there are four mountains and seven access lifts.

Skiing in the East starts with Vermont. (California forged ahead a few years ago to become the Number One ski state in the Union, but its territory is eight times as large as Vermont's.) All Vermont is divided into four parts: the lower, or Bennington cluster; the Manchester cluster; the Rutland cluster; and the upper Vermont cluster.

Jimmy Johnson, former head of Professional Ski Instructors Association, is one of the Midwest's big skiers. His concentration on technique is typical of Midwesterners—perhaps because they haven't got much else to do out there.

The lower cluster, just north of the Massachusetts border, on a latitude with Bennington, centers around Wilmington. It has Mt. Snow as the principal resort, plus substantial lifts at Haystack, Carinthia, Hogback, Prospect, Burrington, Maple Valley, and Dutch Hill. Included in this cluster by proximity are the Berkshire resorts of northern Massachusetts: Jiminy Peak, Berkshire East, Bousquet, Chickley Alps, and Brodie.

Slightly north, on a latitude with Manchester, are Bromley, Snow Valley, Magic, Stratton.

Mid-Vermont, on a latitude with Rutland, has Ascutney, Okemo, Mt. Tom, Suicide Six, Pico, Round Top, and the big one, Killington.

Northern Vermont has Glen Ellen, Mad River, Sugarbush, Bolton, Burke, and, at Stowe, Mt. Mansfield, Spruce Peak, and Madonna. Way up north is Jay Peak, standing by itself, drawing as many skiers from Canada as from the U.S. All told, Vermont has well over forty lift areas, mostly large and prosperous.

And north of Vermont, outside Montreal, are the Laurentians, with Mt. Tremblant as the chief resort and three dozen smaller resorts scattered among the hills. East of that are ten resorts of the eastern townships.

East of Vermont, in New Hampshire, are Cannon Mountain, Waterville Valley—quite new and yet the state's most successful—North Conway, Cranmore, and two dozen more. East of that, in Maine, is Sugarloaf, the king of some two dozen resorts. North from there is Lac Beauport, Ste. Anne de Beaupré, and ten others north of Quebec City.

West of Vermont, in New York State, paralleling the Massachusetts and Vermont resorts, are more than forty Catskill resorts, with Hunter Mountain as the largest. North again, along Lake Champlain, are twenty Adirondack resorts, with Whiteface as the kingpin. (New York has more than a hundred ski areas, more than any other state.)

Taken together, these three hundred lift areas comprise the most extensively developed ski country in North America. They represent the greatest total investment in skiing and draw more skiers than any comparably sized ski region in the United States. Although good figures are hard to come by for Europe, it is likely that there is more skiing done in this 200-by-400-mile region of the U.S. than in the 200-by-400-mile skiing heartland of Europe.

The rest of the East's skiing is in Pennsylvania and the South. Pennsylvania has about fifty small areas, the outstanding ones being Big Boulder and Camelback, between New York and Philadelphia, both with about 700-foot vertical. Camelback has trails more than a mile long. Laurel, in western Pennsylvania, has nearly 1,000 vertical.

New Jersey has ten ski areas, with Great Gorge the largest. Ski Mountain, outside Camden, across the river from Philadelphia, is one of the smallest physically, (140 vertical and one T-bar), but it has a weekend staff of seventy-five instructors teaching like crazy.

The principal facility of the East, however, is not lifts, but roads. The Pennsylvania and New Jersey Turnpikes, the New York Thruway, the Interstates of Connecticut going north into Vermont, the Massachusetts Turnpike—these are the true arteries of the ski industry, and the expansion has accelerated the transformation of a selective, rather snobbish sport into a common, upper-middle-class sport, like golf and sailing.

The weekend is at once the excitement and the bane of eastern skiing. Ingenious plans have to be concocted to secure a ride, to get out of the office early, to beat the traffic, to secure a room, and to arrive at a reasonable hour before midnight. To get enough sleep. To get up early enough. To make it to the lift before the line gets too long. To move around on the mountain from lift to lift. To stay ahead of the burgeoning crowd. To snack at the right time to avoid the crowd at the base lodge lining up for lunch. To avoid the traffic jam after skiing. To get back to the lodge, make a date for an

Preceding pages: The West
has big mountains, big trails,
big snow. Ruthie's Run (l) tumbles
into Aspen from top of Ajax;
Cariboo slopes (r)
have the typical large-scale feeling.
Opposite: Lightest powder is
usually found in among trees, as
at Bell Mountain, Colorado.

Big terrain: Runs at Sun
Valley's Mt. Baldy (l) have the
most varied and extensive lift
terrain of any American
mountain. Helicopters open
nearly limitless possibilities
for skiing powder—in
Bugaboos of British
Columbia (r) and on Mt.
Hayden, near Aspen (below r).
Happy is the skier who
gets out of the "bird" to find
the sun waiting (below).

après-ski meeting, have dinner, and go off to a crowded bar or dance spot for a couple of hours.

And so on to Sunday, with the late risers having to buck long lift lines and getting little skiing if it's a big weekend, i.e., if the snow is any good. Finally, there's the difficulty of balancing how much good skiing is left against the need to get on the road before the mob. Late starters get home at two in the morning and deliver an almost inert body to the office Monday A.M. At one time the inroads on office efficiency made by the joys of skiing the East called forth a countermovement by corporation personnel directors. They began to question potential recruits closely about their interest in skiing. This worked for about six months, until everyone learned to lie a little.

Nonetheless, skiing is exercise, excitement, meeting good new people, and general clubbiness. Skiing is where you meet those it can't hurt to know, now or later. Good friendship and affairs begin, ripen, and sometimes terminate in ski country. It's a college reunion-winter picnic, a great place for girl watching, for business contacts, and for an orgy of physical expenditure that takes the edge off the boredom of the rest of the week.

There's often a hiatus in eastern ski addiction after marriage, but those who are making it soon return, looking for resorts with nursery facilities and a good average between the kind of hill the husband is willing to accept as challenging and the wife willing to endure as the price of togetherness. (Occasionally the roles are reversed.) The really serious start looking for chalets and condominiums, first to rent and then to buy. The kids get their vacations in the mountains at Christmas and Easter, get involved in junior race programs and with skiers of the opposite sex. The lifelines of many families run through ski country.

The sport has become very expensive. A good pair of skis costs $200, two and a half times the price of the best wood ski in the 1950's. To finish off an outfit in top style today requires another $200. The old single-ride lift ticket has disappeared. In its place is the mandatory day ticket with a price tag of $8 and up. (One of my brothers has six children. I have seen him calmly fork over $50 for one day's lift skiing for the family.) A serious ski family with two youngsters expects to spend between $1,000 and $2,000 a year for perhaps five weekends of skiing.

The single person's answer to the expense problem often turns out to be a "ski house." This is rented to one person, the organizer, for the winter at a price set according to the number of beds, usually $150 to $400 a bed. The ski house with ten beds thus rents for from $1,500 to $4,000. The house organizer sells shares and half-shares to a previously committed group of which the full shares will show up every weekend, and the half-shares every other. To dispose of any remaining shares, the organizer then advertises in local papers for "the right kind of people." Typical ads:

"Ski with fantastic people, warm up in a snug chalet nestled against Sugarbush on Rte. 100 in Waitsfield. All for only $400."

"Girls needed—Mt. Snow. Large coed chalet. Nr. slopes. Stereo. Fireplace."

"Need two guys and ten girls to complete large coed house 25 mn. Stratton. 30 min. Killington. Rides arranged. We now have 20 girls, 28 guys."

Group houses buy their own food, hire their own cooks and housekeepers, contract for maintenance, organize transportation for members, sell beds not needed for the coming weekends, regulate guest fees, interest new members through recruiting parties complete with bands and barkeep— a regular weekend commune. The organization goes beyond finances. There's a seldom-breached, unwritten "incest rule": no dating house members. Given the ephemeral quality of most on-the-slope affairs, it makes good economic and social sense to keep house relationships low key.

The group house is not uniquely eastern, but there are fewer in the West simply because it has fewer large rural towns with old homes to accommodate skiers. In the East, once the complex social organization needed to support the group was established, the phenomenon of group housing spread fast. When local housing ran short, the obvious thing was to build chalets designed for group use. The owner reserves his house for himself for a few weekends if he wishes, or he may not use it at all during the winter. Either way, rentals pay most of the running expenses, including mortgage payments. Some entrepreneurs own more than one house and build on speculation, so to speak. The reaction of the natives has not been favorable. Local people stood to profit as long as the old farmhouses being rented were their own. But as new group houses began to fill the towns to overflowing with rambunctious singles, as roadside restaurants and dance joints appeared, the natives were torn between nostalgia and the hope of profit.

The first ski trails cut in the East were make-work projects of the Civilian Conservation Corps in 1933. Thus began the Nose Dive, cut down Mt. Mansfield toward Smugglers Notch, a little north of where the road ran into the farming village of Stowe. There were no lifts on Mansfield. Skiing in the East was strictly a climb and a run. One of the first skiers to climb and run was a young insurance man named Minot Dole—"Minnie" he is called in the history of American skiing. He was an early member of the Mt. Mansfield Club and one of the great organizational influences on the sport. He started the Ski Patrol at Stowe in 1936 and the U.S. Army ski troops in the 1940's; the latter, as the Tenth Mountain Division in World War II, bred a generation of ski executives.

Two other members of the Mt. Mansfield Ski Club were Roland Palmedo and Lowell Thomas. Palmedo helped found Stowe. He later founded Mad River and ran it until he retired. Thomas was already a multimillionaire and a household name as a news broadcaster. When the Austrian cross-country champion, Sepp Ruschp, wrote the Club applying for an instructor's post, Palmedo and Thomas were for hiring him. He came in December, 1936. He put up a rope tow on the Toll House Meadow, and the Sepp Ruschp Ski School "made up entirely of Sepp Ruschp," as *Sports Illustrated*'s Ezra Bowen wrote, "gave 1,000 lessons at one dollar apiece."

Thomas and Palmedo raised enough money to put up one of the newfangled Sun Valley-type chairlifts on Mansfield, and it opened on November 17, 1939. Sepp said, "I remember the date very clearly. It was my birthday. The lift got stuck. There were forty newspapermen dangling in the air for over an hour. Blind snowstorm. We had to pull them down with ropes."

The real making of Stowe began with C. V. Starr, known to his friends as Neil. Probably the richest insurance broker in the world, he came to Stowe to learn to ski. He liked good organization, he liked skiing, and he didn't like waiting an hour and a half to get on the chairlift. So he bought the chair, plus 3,500 acres of the mountain available for the buying, plus the mountain hotel—the works. He put $1 million into new lifts, and built facilities by loan or persuasion. It was the earliest really big investment in the eastern ski world.

Another man completed the job: Thomas Watson, of IBM. He started by buying Madonna, the area on the back side of Stowe's Spruce Peak, and then moved into the Mt. Mansfield Company. The major result was the addition of a gondola, plus a slew of advanced and intermediate trails under it. The resulting total of trails from expert to beginner (with accent on the former), plus the quality of Stowe's terrain—its pitching playfulness—have kept Stowe the standard against which other eastern resorts measure themselves.

The mystique of Stowe has not diminished, even though there are mountains nearly as good nearby. It would be almost unthinkable to be a good eastern skier and not have done such trails as the National or the Starr at least once in a season. Unless, of course, one has been to Colorado or Europe. As far back as I can remember, if you had one trip in your wallet, it had to be Stowe.

What's best about the East is its trails. Much eastern trail design (even before the arrival of Mt. Snow and to some extent thereafter) has been cut to individual scale. Wide boulevards are fine for beginners, but the eastern skier is looking for challenge. The epitome of the challenge used to be the Nose Dive at Stowe—those famous seven narrow swinging turns at the top known as the Seven Sisters. The Sisters have long since been debauched by the bulldozers, but there are many, many absolutely lovely trails still left at Stowe and at Sugarloaf, Cannon, Killington, Jay, Glen Ellen, Mad River, Stratton, and Bromley. Even Mt. Snow found it advisable to cut a set of old-fashioned narrow trails.

The three toughest trails in the East are the Goat Trail at Stowe, the Rumble at Sugarbush, and the Fall Line at Mad River, all in Vermont. These are deliberately outrageous tests, almost indescribable to the western skier who has never seen anything like it. They are sometimes no more than ten feet wide, have nearly right-angle corners, plunge through numbing cascades of moguls (no grooming machine could get on the trails). They are virtually unskiable nonstop except after a good snowfall. They are quickly scraped down to ice and even in the best of conditions become progressively less enticing.

Every top eastern trail has similar—albeit somewhat softened—elements of challenge. The glory of running such trails is not available elsewhere. Cascade, or East Glade–East Fall at Killington, the Lift Line or the National at Stowe, Winter's Way at Sugarloaf, or Paulie's Folly at Cannon—there are twenty such descents in the East that automatically confer impeccable credentials on the skier who can negotiate them in ten minutes or so.

The eastern skier alone knows the deep satisfaction of running a winding, well-made trail, cut with a skier's eye, a trail whose banks and turns coalesce in a fine swooping descent, the exact pattern half-concealed, unraveled at the instant of execution. This magic is made potent by the heavy forest, by the possibilities of the unexpected, by the elegance of performance demanded.

There is more than illusion to this magic. There are approximately two dozen trails in North America which fall into the category of steepest. These are trails—according to *Ski* Magazine—that are more than 3,000 feet long with a gradient of forty percent, or more than 4,000 feet long with a gradient of thirty percent. Of these twenty-four, ten are in the East. This tabulation does not quite do justice to the East, either, since gradients on the upper reaches are much tougher than it indicates. The Appalachians tend to increase in steepness with altitude, forming classic concave sides. The upper pitches of the steepest eastern trails are very steep. The eastern expert can stay away from the crowd by skiing the upper lifts, where there is terrain on which relatively few skiers are comfortable. When you ski the top, you are good.

The pitches of the Rockies tend to decrease with altitude. The Rockies are convex or bulge-sided. The steepest pitches go from midway to the base. The lower lifts are normally crowded with people going up to the top of the mountain; it is not easy in the West to get a day of good steep running.

The top of the Colorado mountains are not exclusive. At Vail the intermediates often take the gondola back down at the end of the day to avoid going over what looks to them like a chamber of horrors—Giant Steps, Tourist Trap, and Prima. Or they detour around them by circuitous traverses. Everybody skis the top.

There are several exceptions to the West's convexity. One is Sun Valley in the Idaho Sawtooth. Its top is as steep as its bottom. Sun Valley's Warm Springs trail goes for 11,000 feet and has an average grade of 30.1 percent, the distance champ of the thirty-percent class (33 degrees). If Sun Valley has an advantage over Aspen, it is that its trails are longer and steeper.

The second exception is Jackson Hole, Wyoming, with the highest lift vertical in the U.S., at 4,100 feet.

Pages 150-151: Powder skier
is a special breed who skis
with his own. His two most
frequent haunts are Sun Valley
bowls, which sit all in a
row, waiting for him, and walls
of Little Cottonwood Canyon
(above) in Utah's Wasatch range,
near Snowbird and Alta.

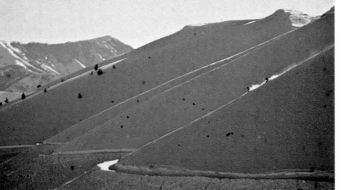

White Frenzy—catching and hard to shake. Its victims—powder skiers—are legion. The song of whispering skis deflects the good man from kith, kin, and steady habits. The only cure is summer—and that's temporary. Allure—of Canada's Rockies (far l), or Sun Valley's bowls (next l), or a cloud of snow—is irresistible.

The top 2,200 feet has a grade of over fifty percent (45 degrees), easily the steepest continuous skiing in the U.S.

The third is Little Cottonwood Canyon in the Wasatch range, outside Salt Lake City. There the terrain is, in a sense, eastern: steep off the top and proceeding down in a series of ever-decreasing pitches connected by run-outs. This is typical of all the terrain at Snowbird, but at Alta, two spurs—Wildcat and High Rustler—reach out and tower over the resort itself. High Rustler is a 1,330-vertical-foot run, with a forty-two percent vertical, close to sixty percent at the top. From there the descent looks like one big jump onto the roof at Rustler Lodge through 3,330 feet of thin air.

The mounds of the Midwest are best described as hemispherical. The most renowned resort of the Midwest is Boyne, with a vertical drop of less than 500 feet, situated on a ridge off Lake Michigan in the northwest corner of Michigan's Lower Peninsula. Boyne is the pioneer glamour resort of the plains, the first to bring chairlifts to Michigan, the first to install a four-place chair, the first to bring in world champions to head its ski school (Stein Eriksen, Othmar Schneider), the first to have a heated outdoor pool, skating, and snowmaking. Boyne Mountain Lodge was built to duplicate the frankly posh atmosphere of European resort hotels. The mountain is on a ridge with a respectable pitch at the top, nice bumpy running where the moguls have been left, and ballroom running where they have been cleared. Six electric chairlifts take some 7,000 skiers an hour up the ridge.

The second most-publicized ski resort in the Midwest: the Playboy Club Hotel at Lake Geneva, Wisconsin. The Playboy Club is more showbiz than snowbiz. Its mountain barely tops 250 vertical, which isn't much higher than the hotel. The Playboy Hotel is just what you'd expect from reading *Playboy* magazine. The imperatives of the Playboy pad are there: the plate glass, the stone, the indoor pools—all shimmering, gleaming, and costing. It's pop architecture, pop décor, and pop sex. The people of Chicago and St. Paul love it.

The hotel is a great family center, with gaggles of kids being towed around by dignified, dressed-up parents. (Lest easterners think this unsophisticated, the scene is duplicated at the Playboy Club Hotel at Great Gorge, New Jersey.) Actually, Lake Geneva works. On the 250-foot vertical quite a few guests learn to ski well.

There's a theory I hold that a beginners' hill should be a small entity of its own with a bottom, middle, and top, all accessible to beginning skiers, and in this way a sort of heartening equality is established. The beginner is not always looking over his shoulder at the Great Peak in the Sky where the ski gods are. This may partially explain the phenomenon of the Midwest skier, who is generally every bit as accomplished as his eastern and western brethren.

The quality of the West that most differentiates it from the East and Midwest is powder. If a region is to have powder—as opposed to just plain snow—in quantity and for a practical amount of time, it must have relatively even temperatures, so the snow will not go through quick changes. It must have relatively open, easy slopes, so the powder will neither run in avalanches nor be wasted in the woods, plus good forest cover to minimize wind, plus relatively frequent, mild snowfalls instead of rigorous blizzard conditions. Lastly, the powder has to come down relatively dry, so it will nest rather than adhere. More than anywhere else in the world, these conditions generally are found in the forty resorts of the Colorado Rockies, as well as those farther north and south, from Taos, New Mexico, through Lake Louise and Banff, in Alberta. To an even greater degree, they are found just west of the main Rockies in Utah's Wasatch mountains and the Interior Ranges (Bugaboos, Monashees, Cariboos) of British Columbia.

Powder skiing is a world of its own. Powder skiers glory in a ski so soft in the forebody that a trail skier would be hard put to control it. Even the politest are called "powder pigs," and the search for untouched soft stuff goes to unimaginable lengths, such as skiing between fallen timbers

or down little twenty-foot shoots just to get to virgin white. I have followed one of Aspen's ranking powder skiers crashing through a tangle of brush and through low limbs dense enough to frighten a weasel, while he marveled at every square inch of fresh powder he managed to cut, and I marveled at the fact that I kept both ankles from being torn asunder and both eyes intact.

These idiosyncrasies do not preclude the discipline of white powder from being so photographed and touted, so advertised, filmed, and written about that, to a nonskier, powder would seem the natural habitat of every skier able to make a turn. It's not. Even in the West there are relatively few powder skiers. Still fewer are those who can ski three-foot-deep powder. Only one in ten thousand can handle the ultimate "bottomless" powder, where only the dynamic forces under the ski keeps the skier from sinking out of sight in the flying froth.

Ski teachers sometimes allege that powder skiing is easy to learn because once the skier is "powder-borne" it's simple and undemanding to make turns. This is like saying that surfing is a snap once you learn to stand on the board and not fall off. Powder skiing demands superior balance and "feel" for the skis, a large dollop of nerviness, and strong legs. The precise elevating and lowering of the long edges of the ski required over the course of a good powder turn calls for extremely subtle shifting of the knees left and right under the skier. (Before the days of the stiff boot it was done with the ankles.) This must be timed to correspond with proper rotary turning motions of the legs and counterbalancing of the upper body. It is also necessary to ski reasonably straight down the mountain, since below a minimum speed the skis tend to sink into the powder and dive, just as in water skiing. Additionally, making a turn downhill in powder is dramatically harder if you are going across the hill rather than angling steeply down the hill. The powder skier is committed to ski right down the steep. His terminal velocity is considerably lower than it would

be on hard snow, but even so the velocity jumps appreciably if the skis "come out" on top of the snow. The best powder skiers try to keep the greater part of the ski in the snow throughout the turn to hold a more stable velocity.

The beginning powder skier, in order to keep his skis from being dragged out to the side, must clamp his knees together and crouch low behind them to keep himself from toppling due to the quickly changing drag of the snow, a drag which constantly varies with the angle, depth, and speed of the skis. The ease with which an experienced powder skier travels—standing straighter and relaxing his clamp a bit—is deceptive. It's an ease built on a system of delicate dynamic balances, something that doesn't show in all those lovely ski movies in which the relatively frequent falls of even good powder skiers have been cut.

Untouched powder is a smooth, floating ride, a fierce kind of freedom, like water skiing down a stretch of white water. Cut-up powder is rougher, less pleasant, and more demanding. The hunting cry, therefore, is "fresh powder!" A standard resort with twenty-four square miles of terrain available may find this considerable acreage slashed to ribbons in a few hours by a couple of hundred experienced powder skiers. Most affluent "powder pigs" have long since resorted to

Acrobatics and Scenery:
The split-position gelandy
holds a skier in stable flight
down toward the wide, placid
waters of California's
Lake Tahoe, which lies below
Heavenly Valley in Sierra Nevada,
one of the four major
ski mountain ranges in the U.S.

U.S. Pacific Coast
has more snow than any other
extensive ski region in the
world. Squaw Valley (r),
where the 1960 Olympics were
held, gets something more than
37 feet. Huge drifts always
pile up on Mt. Baker
(opposite), above Seattle.
Last American trails to see the
westering sun are at Alyeska,
Alaska (above l & r),
not far from city of Anchorage.

helicopter to supply their insatiable demand. There are helicopters flying out to fresh powder in Aspen, Sun Valley, and Alta, and Whistler in British Columbia on every day that good powder blankets the terrain.

Hans Gmoser's operation in the Interior Ranges of British Columbia is the ultimate expression of the quest for fresh powder in North America. Gmoser has two helicopters going all day, sometimes three. There are no lifts here, only miles of untracked peaks and valleys. The effect, both psychic and scenic, is absolutely unbeatable. Gmoser runs Canadian Mountain Holidays in Banff and from there books powder hunts at $60 a day for room, board, and powder. Gmoser's lodges in the Bugaboo and Cariboo are booked a year in advance.

My notes from one notable day I skied in a Gmoser group: "We were now oblivious to any sensation other than the smooth silken susurrus of our skis biting through white unbroken perfection in an undulating series of winging turns through the buoyant sheet of sparkling stuff, a man-deep blanket of soft white diamonds. . . . The snow in the last hundred yards flew to both sides like alternate strokes of angel wings; the tracks were garlands, one ringing the other, as we majestically beat our way down from the sky to our waiting helicopter below on the snow plain."

The best U.S. powder skiing is in the Wasatch, where some 400 inches of powder comes welling over the mountain wall that rises from the plains of the Great Salt Lake, goes over the first tops, and comes down like an intermittent Niagara on the Wasatch's three "destination resorts" —Alta, Snowbird, and Park City.

Snowbird and Alta, standing cheek by jowl in the Wasatch's Little Cottonwood Canyon, are as different as two resorts can be. The atmosphere of Alta's family lodges is reminiscent of New England in 1946. The talk is all skiing, and it's early to bed for the milk run in the morning. There isn't a real night spot in town.

Snowbird is the first American high-rise resort, built on a very limited strip of land a mile from Alta, with a couple of condominium hotels and a large central structure which holds all these: cafeteria, nightclub, bar, steak house, ski shops, and the bottom terminal of the huge Snowbird tram which holds 125 skiers. In between the high-rises, the natural look of the land remains, with tall evergreens and meandering stream almost untouched, the benefit of building in high-rise style.

Park City, Utah, is an authentic mining town catering to skiers. Neither the vertical nor the skiing approaches the great descents at Alta and Snowbird, but the night life is big and unabashed, with a half dozen saloons and a show or two.

Going west to the Coast: One kind of skiing more difficult than powder—and you can get it on powder terrain on those bad days when the snow grains club together in wet masses—is "crud skiing." Crud is also called "junk," or "Sierra cement," an only mildly inappropriate phrase. The skiing on the Coast—in the California–Sierra Nevada and in the Cascade and Coast ranges of the Northwest—is often very unpowderlike. The snowfall on the Coast is greater than in any other place in North America, but a Sierra blizzard coming off the Pacific is unmercifully wet. Having the top chairlift at Squaw Valley so buried in thick goo it cannot operate has happened often enough. Skiing the deep heavy stuff is like skiing dough. In compensation, when groomed, the heavier snow of the Coast packs down into a pleasant, long-lasting base which relatively mild weather keeps from turning into ice. (Nowhere is it as cold as in the East.)

The two capitals of California skiing are Mammoth Mountain, 400 miles northwest of Los Angeles, and Squaw Valley, on the California–Nevada border, 200-odd miles east of San Francisco. Mammoth has a fabulous, steeply falling saddle that has snow along into May, and starts you off from the gondola with a yell and a swoop. The Mammoth saddle is at 11,000. The first thousand feet of descent are treeless, and the next thousand run into great pine groves that lead to Mammoth Mountain Inn, a grand glass-and-stone structure matching the hauteur of the mountain.

Squaw is the only place west of the Mississippi where the U.S. has had an Olympics. The terrain is a complex series of headwalls, steeps, and run-outs, made all the more complex by the fact the Squaw has two dozen lifts, including a gondola, plus a cable tramway that can accommodate more than a hundred people. The Lake Tahoe region has more than 300 lifts all told, the most intensive such concentration in the country.

The Northwest's skiers spread themselves out in some thirty-five resorts in Oregon and Washington, most of them within a hundred miles of Seattle or Portland, or both. The outstanding ski mountains are Mt. Hood in Oregon, and Mt. Baker and Crystal Mountain in Washington. Mt. Hood is an extinct volcanic cone. The massive Timberline Lodge is at the top 6,000-foot level and snow cats carry skiers from 9,000 feet to the top at 11,000. Here there's snow in summer and winter. It's possible to make an eight-mile descent from the top of Mt. Hood to the bottom, skiing through four lift areas. This is the longest continuous downhill on the continent to which skiers are regularly carried.

Mt. Baker's terrain is in much more rolling country, with a short lift of 1,700 feet. But it has six glaciers higher up of sufficient elevation to be skied year round on portable lifts—even though the snow gets a little gray in the summer.

Crystal is the most sophisticated mountain in the Northwest. It has the best-cut, most formidable trails of any resort there, and a Vail-like village at the bottom that holds a thousand people. Most skiers, however, come from Seattle, seventy-nine miles away, for the day. As many as 11,000 skiers inundate Crystal on weekends, an eager horde whose thirst for knowledge is slaked by 140 instructors.

Snoqualmie has the happy distinction of being the biggest mountain near Seattle's population of insatiable skiers. It is only forty-six miles from the center of the city. On an average weekend, the area's chairs, pomas, and dozen rope tows transport some 10,000 skiers several times each up the 1,000-foot vertical. Sixteen independent Seattle schools populate the slope with 5,000 pupils. The picture is unnerving. But it's the Northwest.

To sum up American skiing: The question is, where can it possibly grow without compromising what's already there? The financial and ecological problems of creating large resorts in rural or high-mountain environments have grown more and more stubborn. At least five million people have funneled into snowmobiling, which is just as expensive and, statistically, more dangerous. Tour skiing is absorbing some of the thrust. But the glamour of downhill in the popular mind makes it certain that downhill will continue to grow in spite of obstacles.

Frank Snyder, owner of Stratton Mountain in Vermont, once mused aloud: "Where are we going to put the next five million skiers?" He didn't know. In the West, the answer will be more big hills. There are a few hundred possible mountains, and a few will be wrenched from the grasp of the ecologists. In the rest of the country, where ecologists are strong and remaining mountains fewer and lower (there are only about two economically feasible large mountains left in New England), the answer is "more little hills."

Another answer is an increase in winter vacations to allow present eastern and midwestern resorts to fill during the now-slack midweek period, absorbing a good deal of increase without expanding facilities.

Another part of the answer is increasingly less-expensive air transportation to Europe and across the country, so that Europe's big hills and the West's more sparsely used mountains will take up the increase.

One thing is sure: Americans will continue to ski more, not less.

7

The ski territory of the western world is everything north of the Mediterranean and the Gulf of Mexico, south of Edmonton (in Alberta) and Bergen (in Norway), east of San Francisco, and west of Vienna. This is a big swatch, but not the universe. A great deal—a surprising amount—of skiing goes on outside it. Almost everywhere snow lies, from the Sea of Japan to the heights of Everest, from Afghanistan to the South Pole, someone is skiing on a regular—or an expeditionary—basis.

The largest group of eastern-world skiers ride the Japanese mountains. There are 6 million in Japan alone (one in thirteen of the population), as compared to 4.5 million (one in forty-five) for the United States. Of mountains, as well as skiers, Japan has an excess. Peaks of 6,000 to 10,000 feet stretch for 2,000 miles along the Sea of Japan, facing China. The interior of Japan is mountainous, too. Only about fifteen percent of the land can be tilled, so only snow is required to make skiing possible on the other eighty-five percent. However, the number of resorts catering to Japanese skiers is about 250 compared to America's 1,500. So the experience of the average Japanese skier is claustrophobic enough to be nearly intolerable to a western-world skier. Tokyo alone has a million skiers, and the busiest day experienced by certain department stores is the mid-July ski-equipment sale.

A thousand trains catering only to the ski trade take off every winter from Tokyo's Ueno Station. The best ski resorts are in the Japanese Alps, northwest of Tokyo. As one Japanese described it: "Although more than one thousand ski trains are run especially during the ski season . . . they cannot carry all of the skiers from the city unless the ski passengers are packed in the carriages like so many baggages. . . . The merry skier-goers never mind the crowded trains. Their minds are already on the gelandes [trails]. The passage in the car can become unwalkable because it is also occupied by ski enthusiasts, they they go in and out through the windows. It's just fun for them."

In compensation, the Japanese enjoys a certain economy of expenditure. He can take a late-Friday-night train from Tokyo and sleep en route. The only money he will be required to spend is for one night's lodging and ten cents or so for a ride on the lifts. He will return to Tokyo on Sunday with change from a $10 bill in his pocket, about a quarter of what an American would spend.

The best known of the resorts on Honshu, the main island, is Shiga Heights, seven hours from Tokyo. The crowds on the slope are something else. There's almost no way to turn without hitting someone. The best one can hope for is a narrow miss. Collisions are frequent and inevitable. After each crash, the "merry skier-goers" rise with dignity, bow, and repair minor damage before skiing off again.

Shiga Heights is not all there is to Japanese skiing. There are more sedate, rather delightful resorts, particularly on the island of Hokkaido, north of Honshu.

The Japanese have incorporated hot springs in their after-ski diversions wherever subterranean waters, heated by the earth's mantle, rise through the fissures at the edge of the Pacific plate. Eighty of the 250 resorts have natural hot mineral baths. (You can have a hot-spring bath outside Mammoth, Lassen, and other California resorts on the opposite edge of the Pacific plate, too.) The most famous of the Hokkaido resorts is Sapporo, which held the 1972 Winter Olympics. Sapporo is a large industrial city, but the small villages on its mountains are luxurious. Hot water from the natural springs is piped into large pools, and the guest is given a freshly laundered kimono and tabi every day for after-bath relaxation.

Honshu has two beautiful resorts, less crowded and offering more rigorous skiing than its popular areas. Zoa, in northern Yamagata prefecture, is one. (Photographs of Zao's rime trees are stunning. Moisture blown off the Sea of Japan freezes to rime and turns the trees into monsters.) Another is Mt. Daisan, directly over the Sea of Japan. The skier swoops down the flawless white sides of Daisan toward the

FAR OU

dark blue sea—a marvelous Japanese vision.

Skiing the continent of Asia—for western skiers—is mostly a question of making "first track." This kind of skiing invites hubris and attracts a certain breed, a man who tackles Everest with a climbing team, carrying skis just for the hell of it.

If altitude alone produced skiing, the Himalayas would be the world's biggest winter resort. The range has the only mountains more than 23,000 feet above sea level and, of course, the world's highest peak, Everest, at 29,000 feet. However, human beings have problems acclimatizing themselves to such heights, with their rarefied oxygen, so that the upper limit of feasible lift skiing is around 13,000 feet.

(The highest resort in the United States is at Arapahoe Basin on the Continental Divide, with a base at 10,800 feet and top lift going to 12,500. Other resorts in the western Rockies are built from 8,000 to 9,000 feet above sea level, even though there are higher Colorado snowfields available. The Europeans are much less sanguine about human adaptation than Americans. They build no villages higher than about 6,500, although their lifts occasionally go much higher.)

India's only lift resort goes up 13,000 feet. This is Gulmarg, thirty-two miles from the well-known Kashmiri city of Srinagar. The three-star hotel at Gulmarg, which is actively promoted by the government tourist office, lies at the base of 13,000-foot Aphewat, and there is a 4,000-foot vertical. The slopes hold snow late (Kashmir's temperature is generally cool), and are excellent for intermediates, with a few patches for experts. The clientele is generally international and official, from the "new city" government center at Chandigarh. The runs go up to three miles, an impressive achievement for the only lift system in India.

The only other known Himalayan lift is in Afghanistan at the Chowki Bowl, outside the capital, Kabul. It is much more modest: a 750-foot rope tow with a 240-foot vertical. The auto road ends a few hundred yards from the lift, so porters meet the guests and carry the skis the rest of the way. The interesting thing about the Chowki Bowl, other than that it exists (the skiing certainly is minimal), is that it is just off the old Kabul-Kandahar trade route. Kandahar, by a twist, gives its name to the most prestigious annual European ski race—the Arlberg-Kandahar. The "A-K" first took place in St. Anton in 1928, and was named for the site and in honor of Lord Roberts of Kandahar. The old soldier had won his title by relieving the city during the Afghan war, and in retirement was a sometime patron of international ski racing.

The only other lifts in Mid-Asia, as far as is known, are those presumed to exist at Alma Ata, beyond the Pamir range, in the Tien Shan mountains which form Russia's border with Sinkiang, Red China's westernmost political division. Alma Ata is Russia's principal training site for Olympic winter sports, but its facilities remain something of a mystery; no westerner has reported on it.

Nevertheless, western skis have climbed higher than any others in Central Asia. A notable ascent was made in 1963 by Barry Corbet, a member of that year's American Everest Expedition. He set an altitude record for skis when he took a pair of Head five-footers up to the Western Cwm on Everest. The Cwm is a flat-bottomed, three-mile canyon at an elevation of some 22,000 feet. "One of the thoughts provoked was that we had there the world's finest bunny slope," Corbet reported in *Ski*. "Three miles of gently rolling terrain is not often to be found. It is true that some of the rolls terminate in enormous crevasses. Previous expeditions had advertised snow conditions as good to excellent, since in most years a foot of snow falls each afternoon.

"Great was our dismay, then, to find the Cwm was also having a low snow year. Immense sheets of glittering ice shone between patches of *sastrugi*, or wind-carved, generally unskiable ice sculptures. Add these problems to flat light, the difficulties of skiing with a heavy pack, and the lethargy attendant upon first arriving at 22,000 feet, and it will

Coming down from Coronet Peak toward green fields of New Zealand (opposite), a skier from U.S. has found his faraway adventure. Others ski Antarctica (above), Iceland (l), and an araucaria forest at Lliama, Chile (below). There's nothing unfamiliar about the snow, but the lure of the exotic draws skiers to far corners of the skier's world.

be understood why the world's greatest beginner slope remains untracked."

The next year a veteran climber and Aspen instructor, Fritz Stammberger, took skis 2,000 feet higher in a four-man assault on 26,600-foot Cho Oyo in the Himalayas. Stammberger packed skis all the way, but found the top terrain unskiable. The two other Europeans in the party took sick from cold and exhaustion. Stammberger put his skis on at the 24,000-foot mark and skied nearly 8,000 vertical feet through hellish crevasses to get word to the group below. He risked his life in vain: The two died on the mountain. Stammberger was the only European to survive. He held the altitude record for six years.

Along the southern rim of the Pacific plate are two eminently skiable countries: Australia and New Zealand, both as far south of the equator as western skiing is north. These countries ride the Pacific plate northward and are slated to lose their snow-fields in the tropics in a few hundred million years, and then to get them back on approaching Alaska.

Australia's snowfields are as extensive as Switzerland's but relatively undeveloped. The snowfields lie in the great eastern coastal mountains (somewhat similar to the Appalachians) called the Great Dividing Range. The peaks of the southeastern corner mark the only place where the Australian subcontinent rises more than 5,000 feet above sea level. The rest is flat, flat, flat. Australia's highest peak, Kosciusko, between Melbourne and Sydney, rises 7,328 feet and stands almost in the middle of the cluster known, antipodally, as the Australian Alps.

The notion of antipodal seasons is a bit unsettling. It snows on Aussies from June through November. At Christmas they pick flowers in the Australian Alps. Further, Australia's day is Europe's night. Thus, it's possible that every hour of the day, every day of the year, someone somewhere is going down some mountain on a pair of skis.

The antipodal winter also creates the possibility of skiing on fresh powder the year around by following the snow from November to May in the northern hemisphere and June to November in the southern. A number of western and Australian ski instructors have managed to double their teaching incomes just doing that.

Downhill skiing is older in Australia than in the Alps. Norwegians got there in the Australian gold rush of 1851. Norwegian miners skied for fun and raced for money. The recorded Australian races of the early 1860's were the first pure downhill competition in the world. The Kiandra Ski Club, founded in 1861, predated all other clubs outside Norway. Tintypes of the 1860's show Aussies in work suits and five-gallon hats flashing down slopes, making strong attempts to slow down with the aid of a braking stick tucked under their seats.

As an aside, the Norwegian miners also spread racing to California in the 1860's, racing downhill on huge, twelve-foot skis. The most famous Norwegian skier, "Snowshoe" Thompson, carried mail on a ninety-mile route between Placerville, California, and Genoa, Nevada, by virtue of being the only person around who could negotiate the passes in winter. During the Civil War and until he was put out of business by the Central Pacific in 1869, Thompson was the only wintertime land communication between California and the rest of the Union. It took him three days going east and two days going west—a respectable pace for touring even today. By the 1880's, Norwegians were skiing the mail across the Andes, from Chile to Argentina. But in all these places—the Sierra, the Andes, and Australia—they left no legacy other than a few weathered wooden skis.

In Australia it was not until the 1950's that skiing took hold as a sport. Today several hundred thousand Aussies ski. Not bad for a country so sparsely settled. (Australia, as big as the conterminous [original forty-eight] United States, has only twelve million people, one-sixteenth of

Going up can be as
adventurous as coming down.
Falling backwards down
this wall of Central
European massif
could be quite
unsatisfactory—hence, ice
axe, crampons, and climbing
rope pegged in snow.

Two kinds of escarpments:
Mt. Olympus, in Greece
(opposite)—best admired
with aid of bottle of
retsina, and McMurdo Sound
in Antarctica. Skier is
scientist Peter Schoeck,
who is roped as caution
against gaping crevasses.

Snow lies over a part of
every earthly zone, in some
cases prolonged by underlying
glacial ice, as on the huge
Tasman Glacier of New Zealand
(above). In Africa, the
snow is familiar, but the guide
is not. At Oukaimeden, in
Morocco, he wears a burnoose.

the U.S. population.) Australians are athletically precocious and have produced a good number of top-notch World Cup-class racers, a feat unduplicated by any other nation with such a small base of skiers.

The most highly developed skiing in the Australian Alps is at Thredbo, in Kosciusko State Park. Thredbo has two chairs, more than 2,000 vertical, and Australia's only real ski village. Verticals of 2,000 are hard to find, even in Kosciusko State Park, so that Australia's skiing has to be described as an intermediate's paradise. Thredbo village has a large hotel, a good number of smaller lodges, ski-club headquarters, and a handful of genuine after-ski bars. The hills are smooth and rolling, and dotted with dramatic eucalyptus trees.

New Zealand is much smaller than Australia but has considerably higher peaks. At Mt. Ruapehu, on North Island, a ski lift goes from snowline at 4,000 feet to the 7,300-foot level. To get to the top of Ruapehu—9,000 feet—you walk, passing on the way the crater of the semiextinct volcano that Ruapehu is. There's a lake in the crater heated by springs and warm enough to swim in all winter. In fact, in some parts of the lake the water boils a little. Ruapehu has a six-mile run, among others, and a chance to tour the glacier on Mt. Ngaruho next door. This is a semiactive volcano that erupted in 1954 in full view of the spectators on the lifts. Ruapehu has a splendid hotel for skiers at snowline, the Château Tongariro, offering first-class service for a couple of hundred skiers.

On New Zealand's South Island there are two principal ski resorts: Coronet Peak and the Tasman Glacier. Coronet Peak, near Queenstown, has a 1,500-foot lift to the top of a 5,000-foot summit, the southernmost lift in the world, just 3,500 miles from the South Pole. Coronet stays good and snowy well into spring, at which time you ski above snowline toward a welter of green below, where kea birds and imported chamois and Himalayan thar take cover in the lush foliage.

The most spectacular antipodean skiing, however, is the liftless Tasman Glacier in Mt. Cook National Park. Tasman is an eight-mile run not a whit less fascinating than Chamonix's famed Mer de Glace. A $10 ski-plane ride on the Mt. Cook Airways will land you at 8,000 feet for the long rolling run down the glacier. It's best done in the company of a guide; antipodal glaciers have crevasses as deep as those in the north. On Tasman you are likely to find only three pairs of snow tracks: yours, the guide's, and the plane's. The Tasman is sort of a talisman. Every great ski name has had a crack at it, from Stein Eriksen to Jean-Claude Killy, usually courtesy of Qantas, which is a generous airline, and the only one that flies direct. The Tasman is not difficult. Like most glaciers, when the route is clear, the skiing is easy.

The flip side of antipodal skiing is South America, but in between there is, remarkably enough, some skiing on Hawaii, the largest island of the group, only a couple of hours' drive from sand and surf. Mauna Kea—a volcano—supports the only mid-Pacific ski resort, consisting of Jeep transportation and a couple of rope tows set up at 14,000 feet above sea level. Mauna Kea is fascinating. Half the time the smooth, steep volcanic sides are well above the clouds. But you have to stay attuned to the weather, because if the clouds close in, you had best make for the Jeeps. The Ski Association of Hawaii says: "Sudden cloud changes at any time can reduce visibility to absolute zero. When you cannot see your own knees, you may find yourself helplessly lost."

On the eastern edge of the Pacific basin are the Andes of South America, the world's longest coherent mountain chain. They rise at the Straits of Magellan and extend northward 4,200 miles to the top of the continent. In that length, the Andes have forty-six peaks higher than Mt. McKinley, the highest in North America.

The best-known Andean resort is Chile's Portillo, at 9,500 feet under the soaring 22,834-foot peak of Aconcagua, the highest mountain in the Americas and sixty-seventh highest in the world (after the sixty-six higher peaks of the Himalayas). Portillo centers around El Gran Hotel Portillo, a stark structure in the modern architectural idiom that holds five hundred guests geared to a very posh life style—a requirement that El Gran Hotel Portillo is well-qualified to supply. The cuisine is good, the service superb, and the guests extremely social. Access to the resort is the only thing that is a bit difficult. First of all, there is a limited number of beds, so reservations are best made well in advance. The road is a second barrier. The Pan-American highway from Santiago crosses the Andes here, so it's not that much of a drive—fifty-odd miles, about a two-hour stint—but the pass avalanches more frequently than any other ski resort access-road in the world, outdistancing both the Arlberg Pass in Austria and Little Cottonwood Canyon in Utah by a considerable margin. It works in reverse, too. Lots of people have had their vacations extended by courtesy of the big slides across the Pan-Am highway. It usually takes at least a couple of days to bring skiers out.

The lift vertical is 1,400 feet: lovely, rolling terrain in the middle, and the whole upper part very expert. Two steep, machismo chutes at the top, Roca Jack and Garganta, are superexpert. The terrain is good enough to have a summer contingent of international-caliber racers in attend-

The unexpected awaits on top
of the unfrequented. It can be
a perfect cover of loose,
delectable snow, or a hard windblown
surface, where only a packed
path makes descent a pleasure.
Opposite: Australia's Mt. Buller
(above), and Crackenback
Mountain above Thredbo.

ance, shaping their skills lest they get dull before winter comes.

One visitor reported: "Everybody at the hotel was beautiful. No fat people. No obvious businessmen. People looked like movie stars. Some of them were—stars in ski films. There were lots of twenty-year-old racers, beautiful kids. We were so snowed in that for eight days we only skied the beginner slope, but it was very exciting because we were skiing with the seventy-six best racers in the world."

Santiago is a long day's jet from New York or Los Angeles, and the round trip is double the tour fare to Europe, so Portillo is bound to remain a very special place, worth the price to a select few.

Next to Portillo, the best-known Chilean resort is a twin, Farellones–La Parva, close-together resorts at 7,500 feet on the Pacific side of the Andes. At night the lights of Santiago are visible from both. The biggest lift is at La Parva, a 1,500-foot chair. Most of the accommodations are in private ski clubs.

A third resort area in Chile is Lliama, in the lake country. Lliama has only a bare 400-foot rise to its drag lift, but has one of the world's more exotic settings, right at the edge of a forest of araucaria, a species of tree that grows only at this latitude in South America. Doug Pfeiffer, editor of *Skiing*, described them as "really trunks that rise without taper, without foliage for maybe thirty feet, then explode in a tangle of serpent-like arms covered with sharp-tined, overlapping leaves." If you keep on above the lift you can get to the 5,000-foot top of Lliama, which is an active volcano (part of the Pacific plate edge, again) and has dramatically sulfurous fumes. Accommodations are simple—a *refugio*, or lodge, that takes about 150 people.

In Argentina, the premier resort is Bariloche, near the city of San Carlos de Bariloche and the satellite resort city, Llao-Llao. This is a big, lively resort, but the antithesis of Portillo. For one thing, instead of five hundred hard-to-get beds, there are seven thousand easy-to-get beds. Just

drop in anytime. Less attractively, the beds are all a fair drive from the slopes, except for the Hotel Cerro Catedra, which is right at the slopes of the same name. And not always easy to get into. The main skiing is at Cerro Catedra, off a 2,500-foot chair and 500-vertical lifts on top of that, for a total of 3,000, twice the vertical of Portillo. It's nice, easy skiing.

Bariloche itself is hopping: smart shops, busy discotheques, and so many Brazilians during July it's called "Brasiloche." Bariloche is at 3,000 feet, compared to Portillo's 9,500, so the snow is not so certain, but it is 500 miles closer to the South Pole, and holds snow at lower altitudes much longer.

An extreme of "getting up to get cool" happens in Bolivia at Chacaltaya, an 18,000-foot peak, a thousand miles from the equator on a latitude with Rio de Janeiro. The resort consists of a large stone building, the Raul Posnansky Memorial Ski Lodge, a ninety-minute drive from La Paz, the Bolivian capital. Chacaltaya has a 1,000-foot rope tow and snow all year around. But acclimatization is a big problem, unless you happen to live in La Paz and are used to thin air. You also

have to know the technique for getting a car to the top: Stop at the 16,000-foot mark and pack the space around the radiator and engine with snow.

An even higher lift was once operational on the permanent snow cap of the 19,000-foot Sierra Nevada Ruiz in Colombia, within 400 miles of the equator, but, according to Roland Palmedo (*Ski New Horizons*), it had to be abandoned "because the extremely high altitude limited patronage." Tom Spencer, the last American to report from there, said that although the lift was out, he climbed carefully, with much deep breathing, to ski "some very pleasant windblown powder."

The world's highest cable car is in Venezuela. It is designed for sightseeing, but Spencer took it to the top to ski down under it and make first track, as part of his successful effort to ski the highest peak in every Andean country. The lift goes out of the university town of Mérida and ascends to the 16,400-foot top of Pico Bolivar, which rises from the jungle outside of town. (The rain forest surrounds the tram to the 11,000-foot mark.) Spencer reported, "I had to don crampons to traverse some tricky ice-covered ledges that lead to the permanent glacier in front of Pico Bolivar. Then I skied directly beneath the peak, where the cable car attendants said no one had ever skied before."

It's not very well known that there is skiing in the Atlas Mountains of Africa. But there is, not too far from Marrakesh, the historic desert trading town. The resort is called Oukaimeden, and one of the few Americans ever to ski it was John Fry, the editor-in-chief of *Ski*. "You pass by the camel market," he wrote, "and edge your way through the teeming streets of the old town that has remained virtually unchanged for a thousand years. . . . You do best to stay at La Mamounia Hotel, one of the finest in the world. For around $15 a day two people can obtain a room overlooking an orange grove and a spectacular view of the snowcapped Atlas. . . . Oukaimeden is a winding,

three-hour drive through primitive villages and tiny, exquisitely terraced valleys populated by farmers and Berber sheep herders. Oukaimeden is above treeline, at about 7,000 feet, and the chairlift rises to about 10,000 feet. . . . Powder snow exists in plenty in November and December [but] it was all I could do to get down the hill on my rented, warped skis and World War II combat boots. Bring your own equipment to Oukaimeden."

There's lift skiing in the Moroccan Middle Atlas, and another chair over in the Djurdjura massif in Algeria, but when you've skied the snow near Oukaimeden, you've skied Africa's leading resort.

Between the Atlas and the Himalayas, the only skiing close to thirty degrees north lies at the other end of the Mediterranean, in Israel and Lebanon. Both have mountains with three-month seasons. The Israelis have built a double chair on Mt. Hermon, which has one peak in Israel, one in Syria, and one in Lebanon. The lift is within gunshot of the Golan Heights battleground and has 1,400-foot vertical. A surface lift brings this to 2,000. In peacetime, the greatest danger at Mt. Hermon is from the Israeli kids who slide down the

Far out in the ski world: A gentle trail on Hokkaido (opposite). Japan has six million skiers, more than 250 resorts, and lots of chaos as well as serenity on slopes. Above: Reindeer-jöring in Norway. Northern Lapps may have been the original skiers.

Danger of falling into glacial
crevasses is a hard
fact of high-mountain skiing.
Rescue is as chancy
on Washington's Mt. Rainier
(below) as at Chamonix
in French Alps (opposite).

trails on plastic sheets. They are lethal. The skier may relax from the rigors of skiing Mt. Hermon in the morning by water skiing the Sea of Galilee in the afternoon.

The Cedars, north of Beirut, is the big Lebanese resort. It has a double chair with a 2,200 vertical. The slopes have scores of giant cedar; it's one of the most beautiful ski places in the world.

In Iran there are a few T-bars outside Teheran. In Russia, in the Caucasus, there are several more. Bakuriani, on the south slope of the Caucasus, has lots of touring facilities and a few short lifts at Kochta Gora. But it's certainly not worth the trouble getting into Russia for, unless you want to visit Stalin's early stamping grounds at Tiflis, nearby.

The big resort in the USSR is Itkol, on the north slope of the Caucasus. It lies in the shadow of Mt. El'brus, which tops off at 18,510 feet to make it the highest peak in Europe. El'brus is a stunning giant, an incredible 4,000 feet above the surrounding peaks. In 1966, John Fry rode Itkol's single chair and said that it "had no peer for slowness in the world . . . however, it is blessed by beauty. To the left is a dazzling hanging glacier, to the right a vista of the enormous flank of El'brus." In 1968, the Russians completed a forty-passenger tram to the 15,000-foot level at El'brus for year-round skiing. This ranks as the world's second-highest cable car—after the one in Venezuela.

Turkey has skiing at a resort near the Sea of Marmora, below the Bosporus: Ula Dag, an 8,300-foot mountain in a range south of Bursa, the principal city thereabouts. By virtue of size, Ula Dag was called Mt. Olympus by the Greeks when they owned it, some time back, but *the* Mt. Olympus is on the border of Macedonia and Thessaly. Ula Dag's big cable car goes from the outskirts of Bursa up to the 6,000-foot level. There sits a brace of hotels for skier and nonskier alike. If you ski, you take the lift from here up 1,200 vertical feet. If you have really good snow, you can ski all the way back to Bursa, a good three-mile run, intermediate going, and satisfyingly varied.

A number of nations offer far-out skiing in the vicinity of the Arctic Circle. The honor of having the lift nearest the North Pole goes to Finland. Lake Kilpisjarvi has a drag lift 175 miles north of the Arctic Circle, about 1,300 miles from the pole. But lifts in the Arctic are a curiosity. The serious skiing is Lapland touring. The biggest part of Lapland—a rock, tundra, and forest lowland—lies in Sweden. The rest spreads into Norway on one side and Finland on the other. It's a territory big enough to hold the Low Countries comfortably. The Lapps may have brought skiing to Scandinavia; they still tend reindeer on skis. The ski tourer in Lapland is as likely to meet a Lapp and his herd as another party of skiers. (Luckily, reindeer are gentle.) Sweden maintains trails in Lapland. The principal one is the Royal Trail, 200 miles long, with huts twenty miles apart. Roland Huntford (in *European Skiing*) reports: "It runs among odd, truncated mountains and lake chains, partly above treeline, partly through light forest of stunted birch." The trails start at Abisko, one of the few hotels in Lapland. The Swedish Touring Club makes instructors and equipment available.

Lapland touring huts are sometimes no more than the traditional turf huts, *katas*, and are untended. As in the primitive days of skiing, the skier must bring his own food. Some skiers have their own dog team and *pulka* (light sled) to haul the needed supplies. Others get guides, with pulka included. Spring is the best for Lapland skiing. Weather can be tough other times, even though the aurora borealis is magnificent in winter. Spring temperatures are relatively benign. There's no shortage of light. The day lasts about twenty hours. The terrain runs from the glaciated, rolling, low mountains of Swedish Lapland to the dark bosky pine forests in Finnmarka, in Norway. As Huntford said, "A skier is far more likely to meet a wild animal than a man." Skiing here is like navigating an ocean. The experience may bring on what the

Scandinavians call "the Lapp sickness," an uncontrollable urge to just get out and keep going, wandering through the forests and over viddas that have been standing this way, whitened and silent, since man first put on skis.

All American subarctic skiing is in Alaska. Alyeska, outside Anchorage, roughly 350 miles south of the Circle, has the chairlift closest to the pole, just beating out the chair at Voss, Norway. Alyeska's skiing lies over Turnagain Arm, with a panoramic view of eight glaciers from the sundeck. A double chair delivers 1,200 vertical and some steep terrain reminiscent of Portillo. At the bottom of Alyeska there is the 32-room Alaska Nugget, plus the world's only working carousel at the base of a ski area (to entertain the kids).

An unimportant Arctic country from a skiing point of view is Greenland. A couple of small lifts along the coast are all it has. Greenland has figured in the annals of ski history strongly, nonetheless. The first crossing of the Greenland ice cap was made on skis by the Norwegian, Fritjof Nansen. He crossed in 1888, making the first 240 miles in nineteen days and thereafter finishing successfully. His feat and subsequent book, *Across Greenland on Skis (Paa Ski Over Grønland)* revived interest in the sport in Norway. The book inspired Mathias Zdarsky to take up skiing in Austria, and Kristofer Iselin of Switzerland to found Ski Club Glarus, the oldest in the country. Nansen himself wrote, "I know of no form of sport which so evenly develops the muscles, which renders the body so strong and elastic, which teaches so well the qualities of dexterity and resourcefulness, which in equal degrees calls for decision and resolution, and which gives the same vigor and exhilaration to mind and body alike."

A young Norwegian, Bjorn Staib, duplicated Nansen's track across Greenland in 1962 (others had crossed the cap elsewhere) and then, in 1964, attempted the first ski expedition to the North Pole. Staib's idea was to start in at Alert, on Ellesmere Island, Canada's northernmost Arctic island, 600 miles from the Pole, and traverse the polar ice straight across to Soviet Siberia. He had to quit after reaching a U.S. weather station halfway to the pole, but he had brought skis farther north than any man before him.

Antarctica so far has been skied only by explorers and scientists. The continent is twice the size of the conterminous United States and larger than Europe. It's a strange place. In spite of the popular misconception, not much snow actually falls there—only the equivalent of five inches of water a year.

But what falls stays. The heat of the sun is reflected right back into the sky and there are no warm air currents coming in from the outside. The snow and ice never melt. The accumulated snow (packed into glaciers by the pressure of the top layers) sometimes runs two miles deep to the continental bedrock (actually a series of large islands) unseen below.

The first man to reach the South Pole was the Norwegian, Roald Amundsen. He picked his men for their endurance on cross-country skis. Amundsen and his team skied a good deal of the way. Over the smoother Antarctic terrain a man on skis can make three times the speed of a man on foot, and skis made crossing crevasses on the glaciers safer.

Much later on, an American scientist, Peter Schoeck, took special steel-edged touring skis to the Antarctic, and skied over the Ross ice shelf. He reported: "Skating is what you do here most of the time. Although steel edges may seem strange to cross-country experts, I had good reason to have them. For without steel edges a skier cannot push off when making a skating step . . . the ice is covered only with a thin layer of snow."

Because of Schoeck's mobility, he was fast enough to catch Adelie penguins for studies by the expedition naturalists. Schoeck reported that Emperor penguins were "very puzzled by my ski tracks because they did not cross them right away, but stopped to look to the left and to the right as if crossing a highway—and then rushed across."

Only a few skiers can say they make their living directly engaged in dangerous skiing. But these—amateur racers, big-name pros, stuntmen, ski patrolmen—define the outermost limits of the sport. These are the men who regularly test the human capacity for performance on skis against time, gravity, the hazard of speed, and the dire contingencies of mountain storms, and thereby find their fortune on the snow.

Racers are the most publicized skiers in the world. The natural gymnastic abilities required to become a top ski racer would probably equip an athlete to be a winner in any sport he or she undertook. The tests for which racers train so rigorously are the three classic alpine competitions: slalom, giant slalom, and downhill. These are rather different, a trio of disciplines which only a few outstanding skiers in history have managed to master completely. To dominate all three alpine races during a season, or in an Olympics, is the ultimate achievement. The Olympic alpine triple gold "hat trick" has been pulled off only twice in fifty years, by Austria's Toni Sailer in 1956 at Cortina, and by France's Jean-Claude Killy in 1968 at Grenoble.

Slalom consists of a series of "gates," paired poles about ten feet apart, through which the skiers must pass. Each pair is set at an irregular direction from the preceding one. The racers ski the course, one by one, against time—a mild enough description of what happens. In less than a minute they go through forty to seventy-five gates at speeds of fifteen to twenty miles an hour. It's astonishing that human beings can run such a convoluted route without falling, hitting a pole, or missing a gate completely. To do it a shade faster than the rest of the world's best requires the explosive thrust of a high jumper, the flow of a ballet dancer, and the nerve of a safecracker.

There have been two enormously successful racing families in America: the Werners of Steamboat Springs, Colorado, and the Cochrans of Vermont. Each has placed three of its children on Olympic teams. Mickey Cochran, *père*, has undoubtedly the best record America ever produced, and his appointment as National Team Coach in 1973 was but one in a series of achievements. His daughter Marilyn was the best giant slalom racer in the world in 1969. His daughter Barbara won the women's slalom gold in the 1972 Olympics, his son Bob won the Hahnenkamm in 1973. Mickey Cochran trained his kids on a simple backyard rope tow. His success lay partly in shrewd logic, that to run two to three gates a second fluently the racer has to execute each turn as a wholly subconscious effort—a reflex—because the conscious mind cannot react quickly enough. To condition his youngsters' reflexes, Cochran ran them through several hundred gates a day, every day, all winter.

Giant slalom is faster than slalom. Racers may reach 40 mph. The gates also are set wider and farther apart. Whereas in slalom and downhill, a heroic catch-up effort can sometimes compensate for a mistake, in giant slalom the racer who does everything by the book wins. The giant-slalom winner has to have perfect control all the way. That is, his skis are just enough on edge to make them carve exactly into the right part of the gate. A shade too low or too high in any gate means someone else comes in first.

Downhill is an event unto itself. The season's best slalom and giant-slalom racers often are the same, but the great downhillers are usually not among them. Only an occasional Killy or Sailer has the skill to do all three well. The downhill race is typically run at an average of 55 or 60 mph. This means that at times racers are traveling at 70 to 75 mph, the highest speed at which man on earth travels standing on his own feet. The course is controlled in that there are a few gates. These combine with natural obstacles to define the course—essentially a ski trail with the moguls removed. However, it normally contains large rolls sharp enough to cause the racer to "go airborne" at least a few times along the way. The most exacting skill is required to handle slack stretches with as little drag as possible.

Downhillers try to keep on the snow as much as possible (becoming airborne slows you down), to make turns without undue breaking, and to maintain a low silhouette for minimum wind resistance. Most important of all, they must pick the fastest "line" downhill, given the prevailing snow and weather conditions. The best American downhiller, the late Bud Werner of Steamboat Springs, was the equal of Europe's best. Bud was the first American to win a major downhill in Europe—the Holmenkollen in 1954, when he was seventeen—and the only American ever ranked as the world's number one downhiller in a given season (1959). But his luck was bad. In the 1956 Olympic downhill, ahead of Sailer on time, he fell within sight of the finish. He broke an ankle just before the 1960 games began, and was killed by an avalanche at St. Moritz in 1964. He never won an Olympic medal.

The first two Olympic medals awarded to American men were won in 1964, when Billy Kidd took a silver and Jimmy Huega a bronze in slalom. In giant slalom and downhill American men have failed to win a medal in fifty years of alpine racing. The winners have been the English (very early on) and since then the French, Swiss, Austrians, and Italians.

American women have done considerably better than the men. In 1948, Gretchen Fraser won an Olympic gold and silver at the St. Moritz Olympics, thus becoming the first non-European to rate as the best woman skier in a given season. This was an honor earned, in turn, by Andrea Mead Lawrence of Vermont, who competed in her first Olympics in 1948 at fourteen and won two gold medals four years later at Oslo. Then the honor went to three Canadians: Lucille Wheeler in 1958, Anne Heggtveit in 1960, and Nancy Greene in 1968.

The best male and female skiers of all time, by any objective measure, are both Austrian: Toni Sailer (based on Olympic and world-championship races) and Annemarie Proell. In two seasons beginning in 1971, Proell won more World Cup races (a circuit instituted in 1967, after Sailer's time) than any previous racer, man or woman, and she won the alpine championship combined at the 1972 Olympics, with two silver medals and a fifth. The alltime runners-up are both French: Jean-Claude Killy and Marielle Goitschel.

The evolution of recreational ski technique came about mainly through the adaptation of progressive racing technique. The wedel and the *avalement* are perhaps the most obvious examples. Racers in the 1950's discovered that only skis, feet, and legs had to be turned, and that this "wedel" was much faster than turning the whole body. The racers of the sixties discovered that skis tend to go faster, and that rough terrain handles with more ease, when the skier's weight is back a bit rather than over the boots. The technique of back-weighting first gained fame in the 1960 Olympics, when a French male broke through to the top for the first time in a generation. Jean Vuarnet won a gold in the downhill utilizing the "egg position" (*l'oeuf*) with a low silhouette and weight well back on his skis.

The weight-back position in slalom and giant slalom—*avalement*—was developed later by the French. It calls for rapid shift of the center of gravity over the skis. In short turns the racer "jets" his skis from under him in the turn and gets his weight forward again, over the boots, to finish the turn standing up. This quick back-and-forth changing of the center of gravity was facilitated by a ski with a "beefed-up tail." This kind of ski handles better in a variety of nonracing conditions as well. Today's recreational ski has an afterbody thirty percent stiffer than the forebody. The front of the ski, by older standards, is now made quite flexible.

In the early 1970's, a new kind of alpine race developed, the "pro race," created by Bob Beattie, the former American national team coach. This is a "dual slalom elimination." The racers go down side-by-side courses simultaneously. The first to lose two successive runs is eliminated.

The pro course is set with single

Opening pages: Skier en route to his fortune "through the flags." Young, ambitious racer must have marvelous agility, finesse, and nerve to reach international level where only the super athletes survive.

Whether well-known, like
Poncho McCoy (opposite) or
Gustavo Theoni (far r)
in their time, or obscure
for all time, ski racers all
face the triple trial:
dangerous downhill (opposite),
exacting giant slalom
(double-pole flags), and
intricate slalom dance
(single-pole flags). Only Toni
Sailer and Jean-Claude
Killy mastered all three.

poles rather than double-pole gates, and the racer is required to take the poles on alternate sides. It is somewhere between slalom and giant slalom in speed and quickness of turning. The pro courses have built-in ramps to provide some of the excitement of the airborne moments of downhill. It's a format designed to provide all the visual excitement which has made pro skiing so popular on television. Unlike amateur competitions, in which the best often ski first, the pro race builds to a climax that determines the winner in final head-to-head runs.

The "Nordic side" of competitive sport consists of the jumpers and the runners. The jumper is a sprinter, the man who puts all his effort into a few precious seconds of what—to win—must be flawless action.

The key to winning in a jump competition is to get maximum spring, or kick, off the edge of the jump at the precise moment when the boots pass over it, then to stretch forward toward the ski tips so as to sustain the speed and impulse from the kick by turning the body and the heavy eight-foot skis to aerodynamic advantage—creating a human wing that results in "lift." Holding that form until the last possible moment before landing gives the longest jump and the best form. In Olympic jumping, competitions in which distances are kept under 100 meters, the jumper is rated half on length, half on form. In "ski flying," competitions in which jumps of over 400 feet are common, distance alone counts.

The jumper is never farther from the snow than he is the second he leaves the jumping platform. The landing hill is built to follow the aerodynamic path of the jump so closely that the hill's curve and the jumper's arc gradually come together throughout the jump. (Only the photographer's favorite low camera angle creates the illusion of a heavenward flight.) When he lands, the jumper does a deep, quick genuflection to absorb the impact.

Norway's Holmenkollen hill, outside Oslo, holds the most prestigious annual jumping competition. In the first half of the century, Norwegians dominated all

Racers' expressions range
from concentration to agony.
No one smiles until it's over.
Clockwise from top right:
Professional dual slalom race
at Vail, downhill at
Sun Valley, slalom at Aspen,
elegant giant slalom
by grandmaster Karl Schranz.

Fortune fleeting or enduring:
François Macchi (above), of
1970 French team, and
(l to r) Barbara Cochran, who
won Sapporo slalom for first
U.S. gold in 20 years;
Betsy Clifford, one of a line
of superb women skiers from
Canada; Jean-Claude Killy, the
second man to win three
alpine golds in one Olympics.
Opposite: Britt LaForge (No. 30),
Patrick Russel (No. 11),
Jean-Noel Augert, of the
French team that ruled the 1960's
and early 70's, Billy Kidd
(bottom), first U.S. winner of
combined world championship.

jumping, winning fifteen out of eighteen possible Olympic medals up to and including the 1952 Olympics. Then others caught on. Since 1952, Norway has won only five of a possible twenty-one. The Japanese won all three places in the 1972 Olympic special jump.

The second great division of Nordic competition, cross-country, has in common with jumping only the fact that the heel of the boot is free to rise from the ski. Otherwise, the cross-country racer is the marathon man from any era and any clime, only more so.

Doctors have found that cross-country runners put out much more energy in their longest (thirty-mile) race from start to finish than men do in any other sporting event. The trained cross-country racer is an awesome physical-endurance machine, breathing fifteen times as much air as an average man uses at a standstill. Only superb conditioning keeps a cross-country runner from collapsing under the strain.

The action of a good cross-country racer is an exquisite rhythm. His legs alternately "kick" and relax, functioning in the manner of the good distance runner. Cross-country is a picture of efficient body movement. Nothing superfluous. The skis drive straight down the track, the arms swing close by the hips as they drive the pole back to propel the skier forward, augmenting the kick. The downhill part of the cross-country course is taken straight, except where the track turns. Then the skier makes a skating turn, rather like the primitive turns skiers used in the previous century.

The uphill is the wonder of the cross-country run. The racer goes straight up by a combination of properly waxed skis and strength in the arms. If the wax is appropriately softer than the snow underfoot, the crystals will stick to it as long as there is strong down-pressure on the ski, and will "let go" when the skier springs his weight from the ski and slides it forward. The secrets of waxing are an alchemists's brew. Not for anything will a racer give out his wax combination for a particular day. He wins or loses on it.

The most honored athlete in northern Europe is the one who wins the "Nordic combined"—the best average score between the jump and cross-country. In this age of specialized skiing, the Nordic combined is the only skiing equivalent of the decathlon. Surprisingly, it was here that the only American to win any major European Nordic event triumphed: John Bower of Auburn, Maine, won the 1968 Holmenkollen combined. Usually, American Nordic competitors are happy to come as close as fifth. To win consistently at an international level in Nordics calls for dedication, sophistication, and an ongoing level of competition that never comes together outside Europe.

There is one element of the sport of skiing at which Americans excel, and that is turning a position in the ski pantheon into money. Every great fortune wrung from competitive renown has been made under the direction of Americans, or in America. Today there is more money in the sport for those who merchandise their names. Skiers buy billions of dollars' worth of advertised goods and services each year. The man who can sell himself as a brand's standard-bearer can make a good living. The most notable example, of course, is that of Jean-Claude Killy, who, under the direction of International Management, turned his three Olympic gold medals into $1 million in the United States in three years. By contrast, Toni Sailer, who operated mostly outside the United States and on his own hook, turned three gold medals into a small hotel in Kitzbühel—no more.

An Olympian can make fame last, provided he takes care of his image. Norway's Stein Eriksen won the world championship in 1954 and has earned more money every year since. He did things right. First, he came to America immediately after he'd won. And, second, he has been continuously visible as head of prestigious ski schools (Boyne, Sugarbush, Aspen, Park City). He also was the first to stunt-ski extensively for films. And he, too, is handled by IM.

Top: Willy Schaeffler (1) directed
1960 Squaw Valley Olympics; the late
Billy McKay contemplates course. Middle:
Michele Jacot (1) on a winning day;
Anderl Molterer and Stein Eriksen,
stars of the 1950's. Bottom: Schranz hears
he is disqualified, Killy that he
has won a third gold, 1968. Russel (far r)
vaults exuberantly through gate.

"The Flip": Although Stein
Eriksen showed the way,
it was skiers like Hermann
Goellner (above) and Tom
LeRoy (with Hermann,
arms crossed, at right) who
achieved multiple flips
that made for such
awesome entertainment.

A most dangerous path to ski fortune was devised at the turn of the 1970's. This was the "first descent." One man practically singlehandedly brought this awe-inspiring category into being. This was Sylvain Saudan, a Swiss guide and instructor, a balancing nonpareil, a spitter-in-the-eye-of-danger, the conqueror of unbelievably steep, dangerous, previously unskied descents. In the course of a few winters, he skied down the Eiger, the Gervasutti, the Bionassy at Chamonix, the Couloir Marinelli, and the Grande Jorasse. These places are so steep that climbers have been killed trying to go *up* them in the summer!

Saudan was the first Steepness King of Skiing. Indisputably. His preferred zone of operations was the narrow *couloir*; the ice sheet; rock-strewn, wind-blown, impacted snow; deep, gooey junk; brittle, treacherous, breakable crust. Saudan liked it tough. He skied anything. He didn't fall. And he lived. The owner of Hotel Skilt at Les Menuires once described Saudan:" *Fou.* He is *complètement fou.* Crazy. He has to be."

However, this was not so. He skied quite slowly, resting between sets of turns. He made two thousand turns on an average descent. At least the first thousand had to be perfect. One miss and he'd slip and start an avalanche and bury himself, or fall a thousand feet. Yet he is so sure of his way of skiing that he plans to die, he says, "at age one hundred in my bed." He may well. Edmond Denis, head of the ski school at Avoriaz, comments, "First, Emile Allais taught us the *ruade,* how to turn about the tips of the skis. Then James Couttet taught us how to turn the ski under the foot, in the middle. Now Saudan shows us how to pivot the skis at the tail."

"When you turn on tails," Saudan once said, "bad snow can't stop you." He's pretty much proved it. Any number of skiers have the technical expertise to do Saudan's descents, but only two or three have had the incredible confidence that makes Saudan's runs possible.

Stuntmen on skis are a creation of film. Robert Redford, actor, director, skier, used a stuntman to create the first creditable Hollywood ski film, *Downhill Racer.* There was a top ski stuntman in the 1971 James Bond film, *On Her Majesty's Secret Service.* But the original stunt-film company, Summit Films, a Colorado firm, practically created the category. Nearly every season, beginning in the late 1960's, Roger Brown, head of Summit, took the stuntmen signed with Hart Ski Company into the French glaciers above Chamonix. Summit made five ski-stunt films in five years, all famous on the ski circuit, including *Outer Limits, Moebius Flip,* and *The Great Ski Chase.* Hermann Goellner and Tom LeRoy, two of the Hart stuntmen, became the first skiers in the world who could flip three times in the air on skis. (The third man who learned broke his back doing it and died.)

For a triple, you have to get at least thirty-five feet into the air while going forty miles an hour. Then you do three flips—airborne somersaults—with skis attached to your feet. If you come out too far forward or too far back, if you are not within ten degrees of horizontal, you won't recover. Even top stunt skiers make mistakes. Bill Peterson, working in *The Outer Limits,* flipped off a cliff, misjudged his arc, and landed in the top of a twenty-foot tree.

Stuntmen ski under continual threat of avalanches. To ski in beautiful powder snow for films, you've got to go where there is avalanche. Tom LeRoy sometimes deliberately set off an avalanche and skied the snow wave for the beautiful picture effect.

Glacier shots are typically done in a jumble of huge, towering seracs where—in between—the snow is as hard as glass. Stuntmen climb this dangerous stuff for two hours to ski down one little stretch.

Glacier crevasses are three or four feet wide at the top and narrow very slowly to a depth of some hundreds of feet. Blowing snow builds bridges across the crevasses. If you ski the bridge at the wrong angle, or with too much weight, it collapses. Skiing a clear, virgin snowfield, you

Fortune does not always smile on nerve! A luckless hot-dog contestant at Vail finishes his one-and-a-half gainer—or whatever it was intended to be—without skis which have fecklessly abandoned their young owner in mid-trick.

Mature free-styler has a repertoire of leaps, side wiggles, ski crosses, and Rorschach ink-blot figures that leaves viewer breathless. Jeff Jobe (below) began a craze with his flying kite wing which floats him, skis dangling, from mountaintop to bottom. If he does everything right, he lands gently on snow.

suddenly drop into a crevasse. Tom LeRoy once skied into a hidden crevasse at Chamonix and hung by his arms until the rest of the crew got to him and pulled him out.

LeRoy did the most spectacular of all his leaps over a man-made bump at Vail. He hit the bump going sixty. He cleared a little tree, two forty-foot pines, a rope tow, a road, and the whole group of stuntmen, six other skiers who had stopped and were looking up. LeRoy even cleared the movie cameraman who was waiting for him. He went more than 400 feet. He landed and kept right on skiing.

Stuntmen are goaded by the mere existence of others, and pressured to take more chances and more chances. Another part of their motivation is simple ego. They enjoy the fame and being in films and hearing people talk about them: "Did you see that jump? Did you see what he did?" And they can make money doing it. The average deal is to sign with several major sponsors at $10,000 a year, plus $100 a day for appearances or filming. The stuntmen are all paid by at least one ski company and one boot or binding company, with extra fees for endorsing poles, skiwear, an airline, a liquor brand, etc. Stunt skiers have to take the same chances as a regular Hollywood stuntman, and be able as well to stand up and give a speech at public-relations functions.

LeRoy, like all stuntmen who are good, simply doesn't register sharp, impending danger, no matter what situation he is getting into. On one day of filming, he lost control and ran head-on into an ice wall. He shook himself, got up, and went on to jump across a gaping crevasse.

Several of the most astounding stunts of the century have been pulled off using mechanical aids above and beyond normal ski gear. The prize for altitude went to a Japanese racer, Yuichiro Miura, who strapped a braking parachute on his back and schussed the south slope of Mt. Everest. He took a large Japanese expedition in 1970 to the 26,000-foot level of Everest and then turned around and pointed his skis down. He went straight for a couple of thousand feet, then pulled the rip cord. The parachute deployed. Nothing happened. Miura rocketed on. The air was too thin to let the chute brake effectively. Miura was headed—at something like 100 mph—for a great crevasse. He seemed unable to throw himself to the snow. Miura's chute suddenly caught a gust and pulled him off his feet. He slid straight toward a boulder, struck it squarely and flew into the air, coming down with an audible thud barely short of the crevasse. He lay still. Then he became conscious enough to wave a ski pole at the horrified watchers below. He had survived.

The second stunt also involved a chute. Rick Sylvester, a ski instructor at Squaw Valley, decided to jump off the 1,000-foot face of El Capitan, the rock tower in Yosemite Park. He planned to ski off, free fall, and then parachute to safety below. He spent all summer learning how to sky dive. Then, with a camera crew filming, he helicoptered to the top of El Capitan, where the crew built a ramp to the edge. He shot down it and took off. The onrushing air hit him in the chest. He somersaulted backwards, end over end, trying to pull the cords attached to his legs that would release the skis. He finally got rid of the skis, still tumbling, and with the ground coming up fast pulled the rip cord. The chute opened—not a second too soon. Sylvester landed in the top of a pine. He was dissatisfied with the pictures that were shot. He went up a few weeks later and did it again and got better pictures.

Jeff Jobe invented a man-carrying glider wing that enabled him—after much rehearsing over water —to take off from a slope on his skis and fly the rest of the way down the mountain hanging in the wing. It was highly risky. All Jobe had to do was to mismanipulate the kite and lose lift and he'd drop all the way. (Several later kite fliers with copies of Jobe's kite wing were killed outright.) Jobe broke several bones in a crash when he tried to fly his kite wing over a mountain in summer. The thin summer air did not give enough lift.

The "figure skiing" phase of the sport now has taken off. The 1972 tabulation of possible tricks and

Most awesome of Nordic
disciplines is the ski
jump. As the hill falls
away under him, jumper keeps
dropping—up to 400 yards
in big jumps. Camera angle
can make jumper look high
or, as here, about to auger
in, which is unusual.

A good cross-country racer
is a study in economy of
motion, belying the enormous
physical output required
to maintain unflagging pace.
Cross-country demands
more endurance than any other
sport in the world. Jumper
has an aesthetic of balance
with which to overcome
vagaries of wind so
that he lands precisely,
in a supple genuflection.

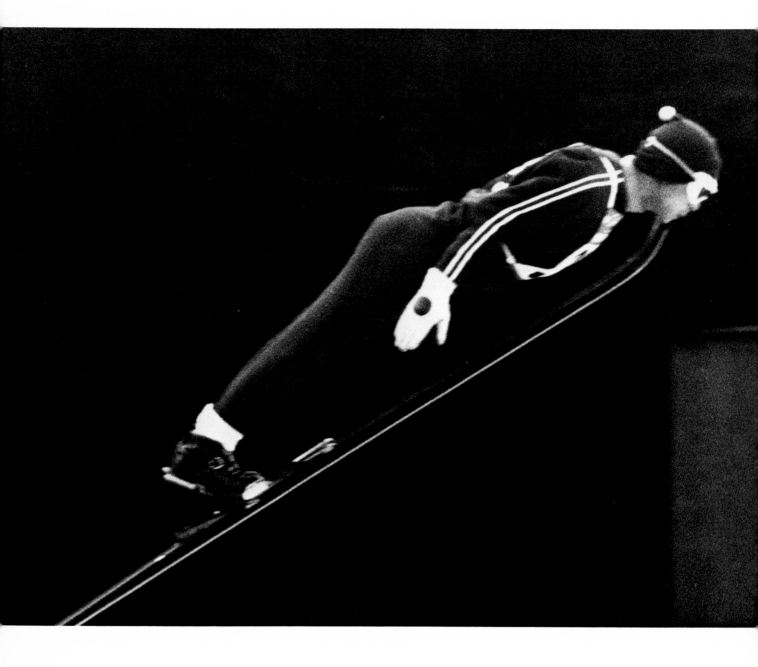

The essence of jumping
is the position of the jumper
in the air. He must, as
the Japanese jumper here,
pitch far forward so that his
body forms an airfoil to
gain maximum distance from the
takeoff—a human wing, in
effect, gliding down to earth.

figures compiled by Matt Broze in his book *Freestyle Skiing* counted 70-odd maneuvers that the Compleat Figure Skier has to know. A pro Hot-Dog Circuit was established with prizes going as high at $5,000 for first place. At least a half-dozen crazy skiers almost make a living at it every winter.

Ranged alongside the Hot Dogs (who tend to go flaky in looks and lifestyle as well as skiing style), the ranks of the Ski Patrolmen and Avalanche Patrolmen seem to be made up of World War II bomber crews with millimeter haircuts and battle uniforms. But the glory and the heroism is there all the same, and the risk is sufficient to be interesting.

The basic ski patrolman is someone who can bring a rescue toboggan down a steep, mogully trail without untidily jarring the occupant—the accident victim, that is—lying in the toboggan. An out-of control sled could compound an injury.

(The apocryphal story about the Ski Patrol is the one in which the patrolman loses hold of the sled. It goes down the slope solo and turns over. The victim slides to a stop. The patrolman comes flying down, rights the toboggan, pushes it toward the victim who, with a cry of fright, rises from the snow and starts running down the mountain, with the patrolman in hot pursuit.)

Minnie Dole, who started the Ski Patrol, tells a true story of a time he struggled for an hour to sled a presumed victim down the two-mile Sherbourne Trail on Mt. Washington. Minnie finally came to a hard-breathing stop in front of the hut at the bottom. The man got up, dusted the snow off, thanked Minnie and walked into the hut.

The making of a patrolman can be painful. The art of toboggan handling is treacherous. In one class of patrol candidates at Stowe, where the patrol is super-professional, nine passed, four didn't, and three broke bones before the course was over. All were good skiers to begin with.

The Avalanche Patrol member is a combination of a ski patrolman and a Forest Ranger. It is largely the outgrowth of the work done by Monty Atwater as a U.S. Forest Ranger at Alta after World War II. Atwater found ways of triggering avalanches on command by throwing hand-held ignited dynamite at the right place on the slope at the right time of day. Once a slope has slid—or failed to slide—it is safe for skiing, generally speaking. Monty also learned how to trigger avalanches by cutting the snow with his skis at the very tops of hills, thus creating a snow fracture that caused newly fallen snow to avalanche immediately. Monty eventually took to using howitzers, recoilless rifles, and a king-size air gun to hurl explosive shells up onto slopes to make them avalanche on command. After that the Patrol skis the slopes first—to prove they are safe.

By the 1960's, Monty far surpassed the traditional European system whereby an area is "closed" by posting a simple sign or two and waiting for a natural avalanche to make the slope safe again. It is well that Monty pioneered the practice of opening powder slopes immediately after a storm, since American skiers were too impatient for the European kind of "control." Big western resorts all depend on the Avalanche Patrol to keep their powder slopes open. Otherwise the slopes go to waste, packing down into windblown drifts not very much fun to ski.

The U. S. Forester or ski patrolman on the Avalanche Patrol has undergone training that includes making up and throwing hand charges, cutting off cornices with his skis, and manning requisite artillery. It's not a job for the nervous. One of the Alta Foresters in the 1960's was cutting a cornice with his skis when it cracked open behind him. His rope, belayed by his partner, was severed by the icy crust. The Forester traveled a thousand vertical feet under the snow with the avalanche. When it stopped, all that was showing was his glove. Luckily, a skier had been watching. He came over fast and dragged the man out. The Forester retired quietly to a desk job. But others remain to keep the white torrent at bay for skiers, making powder skiing the only sport that depends on artillery to keep it going.

Skiing is, besides skiing, celebration and carnival, sweet relaxing, ego-clothing, accoutrements, fashion and technology. Taken together, these satellite satisfactions put the finish on an eminently satisfactory whole, a good life better than the real world's. "Après-ski" is the phrase that best carries the import of the extras. The fireplace, the hot buttered rum at the inn with mine host hovering, solicitous—to some this is still the meaning. But the soaring popularity of skiing has given the term a multiplicity of new meanings. Après-ski now connotes special trysting places, sophisticated bars and boîtes, and a full-blown consumer economy in fun, fashion, and equipment.

One essential of it all, however, is simple and unchanging: boy-girl, boy-girl—the magic of attraction. Add to boy-girl power the adventure of being away from home, the excitement of sharing and conquering common dangers of gravity and snow, and a ready-at-hand intimacy.

The snowballing après-ski has created scintillations ranging from the wonderful to the dubious. Among the wonderful are the sun porches of Avoriaz, the tea dance at the Tenne in Kitzbühel, an Old-Fashioned sent up to your room when you come back to the Lodge in Sun Valley, hot mulled wine in the Blue Ox at Timberline Lodge, sitting in the sun at the bottom of Little Nell in Aspen, lunch at Les Menuires' Châlet de Neiges, which may include cassis, country ham, omelette with smoked pork bits, blueberry tart, and a heady local liqueur called kir. It's apfelstrudl at Gerdas in Tourtellote Park, a beer sparkling at the Gold Coast high above Squaw Valley. It's watching the nicely turned-out girls come into the Chesa Viglia at St. Moritz, the teeny boppers at the rock matinee at the Wobbly Barn in Killington. It's the instructors hunting at the Blue Tooth.

It's boy-girl, boy-girl. It's the whole mountain full of side-by-side chairs, two-by-two T-bars, and a liftline shoulder to shoulder.

Girl-watching is an après-ski occupation and Stowe is the East's girl-watching center. The flood of nubility rises to a climax in spring, when the colleges turn out for the between-semester week. Notes from a girl-watcher: "Stowe's are quick, bright Eastern girls—their fathers are lawyers in Boston, insurance men in Hartford, account men on Madison Avenue. This has nothing to do with the shape of the girls, which is good. The girls stay in wonderful humor as long as treated well in making an appeal—a certain graciousness coupled with a lack of pretense is held admirable in the East. The girls make no promises, except in the bright, engaging laugh given so freely. It is spring, after all, and the winter is nearly over."

Western girl-watching centers in Aspen. Handlebar mustaches and girls' long, straight blonde hair appeared in Aspen at a time when the rest of the country was divided between National Guard haircuts and beehive hairdos. So love in Aspen has always been far ahead. Being in love in Aspen is even more important than just being in love. That's why there are so many girls in Aspen. The girls share everything but men. Because Aspen is expensive and rooms scarce, the girls live four and five to a condominium apartment. Aspen's Beautiful People are not the moneyed but the young, whose lifestyle has been so widely copied.

But being Beautiful is not always easy. A "hippie war" raged in Aspen in the late sixties between the established proprietors and the Beautiful People. Basically the cause was a confusion in the minds of the proprietors. In summer, kids at Aspen could be, and often were, committed to indigence. But the winter Beautifuls were girls and guys as ambitious and structured in their own way as the Establishment. The young person in winter Aspen comes from a fighting upper-middle-class background, at least. By the time the season has started, every scarce job and spare bunk has been wrestled for and won by the aggressive Beautifuls. And they also set the after-ski scene, defying attempts to discourage their presence (which Vail had been able to do successfully).

Aspen's "Battle of Guido's" was the

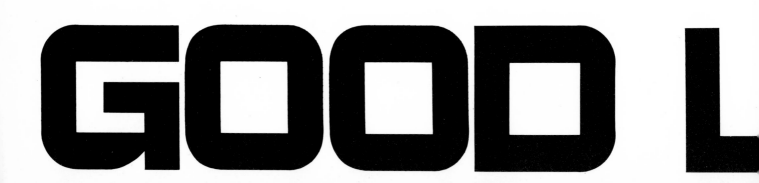

GOOD L

IFE

Skiing is an egalitarian
sport as regards the sexes.
More than any other
it gives women a parity with
men in sharing mutual
exhilaration. Taking a
simultaneous descent
(above) creates nonsexist
camaraderie on the slopes.

Skiing requires
relaxed, fit muscles and
a certain élan to
execute well. It is most
fun for the physically
energetic. Skiing
thus has an attraction
for the already
attractive, buoys the
buoyant. It is
a sport of high spirits
and uncommonly
handsome practitioners.

Après-ski is a magic
phrase, conjuring visions
of excellent fireplaces
—this one at Avoriaz—
a hot drink,
genial companions, and
the languor that
eases the strain of
a long day's runs.

symptomatic struggle. Guido's was a fine, traditional Swiss restaurant, owned and directed by a Swiss. In the 1950's you needed a reservation to get in. Then Guido declared war on the Beautifuls. He refused to serve males with long hair. He engaged in political maneuvers on a municipal level to try to force the Beautifuls out of town. The strategy backfired. No Beautifuls, no customers. Today Guido's is a fine, traditional Swiss restaurant, and you can walk in any time, long hair or not. Guido himself has left town. The war is over.

The Aspen Beautifuls are not quite so far into the work ethic as the Establishment. They have more fun. They give Aspen's après-ski a zip that keeps it on top as *the* place for après-ski in America. And while the Aspen Beautifuls are a product of the American fantasy, just as the bronzed St. Moritz jet-setters are of the European fantasy, Aspen's good life is yeastier, more kaleidoscopic, with more fantasia, more blithe spirit, wilder dancing, and freer skiing than that in any European locale.

Europe reaches the heights of Aspen's social life only in Austria and Germany during *Fasching*, a Mardi Gras more extended than the New Orleans version. In *Fasching*, Germans let go and make it terribly gay—if it takes two weeks without sleep to do it.

Fasching is your own party and other people's party. One night you and your best friends have a gala. On others, you attend the galas of other friends, and that's quite a round. The first time I saw *Fasching* was in Garmisch. I was sitting at the dance floor of the Alpenhof having a drink, watching the sedate dancing. Then the *Fasching* people arrived, about twenty—young, old, in-between—stunningly turned out, some in costume and some out. The line was hard to define. They brought their own toastmaster. They took over the microphone and the dance floor shook. The pace of the evening accelerated. Girls invited boys to dance, a guest took over the bandleader's slot. The rules were off. One group turned the evening upside down, and this happens in *Fasching*.

Fasching in North America is Quebec's *Carnaval*, the French-Canadian Mardi Gras. The big action is in Quebec City: torchlight parades, snake-dancing in the streets, three weeks of planned brouhaha which spreads in spirit to all seventy-odd ski areas in the Laurentians.

The Laurentian scarp is a very old, ground-down set of mountains. Ninety percent of the verticals are under 750 feet. Only Mt. Ste. Anne, outside Quebec City, and Mt. Tremblant, outside Montreal, have verticals over 2,000. No lifts reach 2,500. (To get that kind of vertical in Quebec, you would have to go out on the Gaspé, in the Chic Choc Mountains, where Quebec's highest peaks reach 4,000.) What the Canadian French lack in altitude, however, they make up for in attitude—*ésprit* with a *soupçon* of madness.

The St. Sauveur scene: "On weekends, the resort is easygoing, boozy, and charged with verve," wrote Peter Miller. "Everyone's here: French families, racers, the Montreal society set, teen-agers, fashion models, and the *drag-geurs* who drag girls around St. Sauveur in their fast cars. There is also French-French food, French-Canadian food, pizza, plain food, discothèques, bawdy songs. The best description of St. Sauveur's *fin de semaine* came from the lips of a swinging, exhausted Gallic beauty, 'It's one big indoor-outdoor discothèque.'"

That goes double during Carnaval. "The strenuous grip of winter was broken and the floodgates opened," wrote Kim Massie, who photographed a recent Carnaval. "The enthroned Queen of the Carnaval and her court . . . in the cold, riding floats down the floodlit streets . . . may have had heaters hidden under their dresses, but they were brave from the waist up." Ah, the French. Even in Quebec.

The closest to Carnaval in the United States is Aspen's Winterskol. It has the requisite parade and high jinks. But Americans are much more talented at more spontaneous happenings—parties during Airline Week, when a ski town is jammed with stewardesses, and at lunatic cele-

For young or old,
après-ski means music and
friends, an ambience
as recognizable in Vermont
(above) as in Aspen
(r), or France (second r),
or Vail (top). The
call of Rock (far r)
mostly summons the young,
the only humans with
so much surplus energy
to spend after
a long day of skiing.

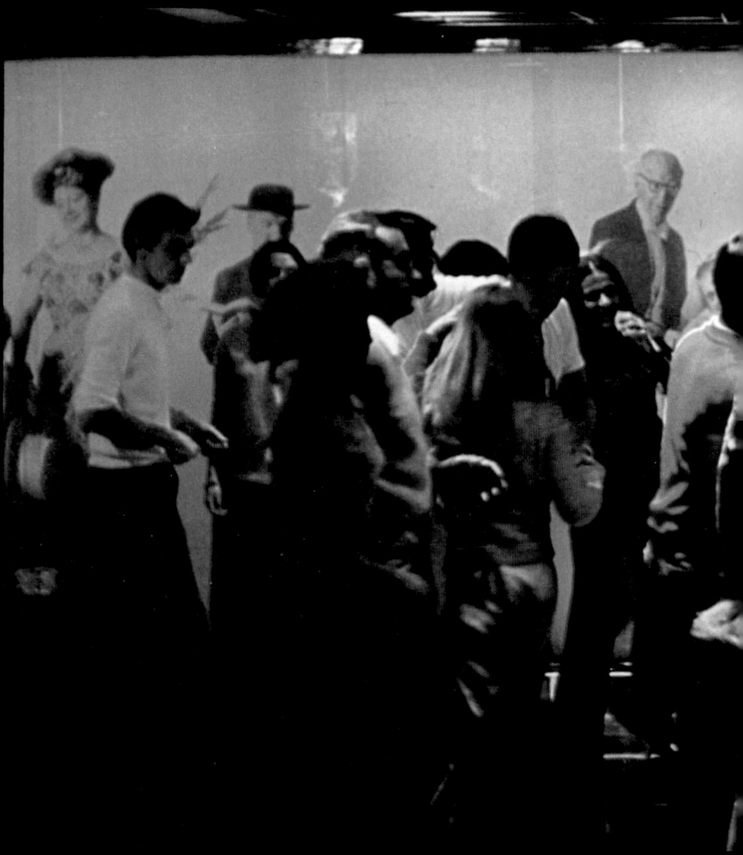

The comfortable, enveloping relaxation of après-ski takes many forms—music and good drink, good company, warm food, and sun at a restaurant on Gold Coast slopes of Squaw Valley; in a heated swimming pool *à deux* at Vail; preparing a ski tourer's meal on a frosty day at a mountain shelter in Vermont.

The good life: a deli at Les Arcs (far l), hot, mulled wine anywhere (above), a welcome cup in Vermont (l), and just taking it easy in lodge at Alta (below). It's *de rigueur* to appreciate styles off slopes as well as on. If you have to ask what après-ski costs, you really can't afford to ski.

brations such as gelandy contests, hot-dog contests, ad hoc beauty contests, and the berserker days of the spring slush races.

Gelandy, or *Geländesprung* (from German *Gelände*—terrain, and *Sprung*—leap), contests were truly amateur and spontaneous events in the 1960's. The sight of a ski buddy sailing off an informal bump into an informal crash-and-burn was good for a whole night of celebration. In the 1970's, gelandy contests were regulated. A gelandy circuit was founded, but still the event is preceded at night in toasts to the morrow's victors and to the losers-to-come as well.

Spring slush races are slaloms with the finish line in a melt pond, the visible funeral of the winter. A hilarious wake is had by all. The chain of cold has snapped, the goal of being really better on skis this year is unachieved. The skis have become scuffed, the stretch pants replaced by ragged short jeans; it's sap-rising and slush-raising time at the old slalom run. It's the good life.

But all this is the experience of insiders, and it takes a certain amount of effort and élan to get to the in-side of skiing. What of outsiders? Do they have a good life? The good life of the bus-to-Mt. Nowhere crowd is not sublime. Here is an eye-witness account of mine from *Ski*.

"Mt. Nowhere is that impossible mountain of the mind . . . where all the siren songs of ski-resort publicity ring true. It is the fabled resort where there is always an exactly equal number of boys and girls, where there is a perpetual light dusting of fresh powder, where the sky is blue all day. The temperatures at Mt. Nowhere range from invigoratingly cool in the morning to just warm enough for suntanning in the afternoon. Surrounding this happy resort are establishments offering glorious and never-ending after-ski diversion from which the skiers of Mt. Nowhere arise like the warriors of Valhalla, refreshed and ready for the joys of the hill."

Who believes in Mt. Nowhere?

"The semiperennials of the sport, the neophytes, the draftees, green and willing. They are the people who move in and out of the sport with such rapidity . . . a generation of wide-eyed novices who pile on buses and jam into snowtireless cars borrowed for the weekend and arrive . . . well, they just arrive, that's all, with arms out, saying 'Show me that marvelous time, like it says.' "

In the course of the weekend, the advertised "ski lodge" became a downtown hotel in Rutland, and the instructors a group of pickup skiers who came along for the ride (and pickups). The snow was icy, the skiing lousy, the after-ski a few moments at a bar where someone sang a few songs on a guitar. But they kept the faith.

"They may have been green two days ago, but now they are blooded in their first battle for Mt. Nowhere. As we roll into the Bronx somewhere around midnight, I hear the next day's rehearsed office conversations. Ski instructors will be eulogized, Saturday's songfest will be built into a bacchanal, and another round of stories will thus resound to the greater glory of the legend of Mt. Nowhere."

Let us turn to a wholly different bus trip, one that had a superorganized good life, an 800-miler with the Space City Ski Club of Houston, Texas, to a goal whose joys were known: Sierra Blanca, where the Rockies subside into a line of low hills above the dry plains of West Texas. Sierra Blanca is 12,000 feet high and it always has snow.

Texans are a radical come-lately phenomenon in the sport. "The bus drew away amid happy shouts and, inside, the social machine found its parts. They meshed and the whole revved itself effortlessly into a ring-a-ding party. By the time the bus had turned the first corner, a well-stocked bar had been rigged at the rear of the cabin and varieties of mixed drinks were being proffered almost magically. In the middle of the cabin, a group was already singing softly. Texans passed and chattered over the pleasant hum of words and music, changing seats as if by telepathic signal. No one was

Good clothes are part
of the good life. Be
dramatic, be different.
This is the sport
that encourages you to dress
like a circus aerialist
and limber up in public.
It's fun, it's distinctive,
it's expensive.

left out. Inside we were a self-sufficient, well-conducted hive of king-size bees, all rubbing antennae and signaling by the very intensity of our buzz that all was great."

At Sierra Blanca: "They cleared away the benches and set up a frug floor. It was as if the snow was still 750 miles away. But when afternoon came, the Texans got out on the snow. And ski they did, as best they could. It was awesome."

The Southwest, under the influence of Texas, may be where the good life will undergo its final metamorphosis. There are three destination resorts in New Mexico —Taos, Sierra Blanca, and Red River. There is also the U. S. resort closest to a large city, Sandia, with a cable car rising right out of Albuquerque. (Grouse Mountain in British Columbia, with a tram coming right out of Greater Vancouver, is the only other similar North American situation.) New Mexico also has Cloudcroft at Alamogordo, started by the atomic scientists engaged in the White Sands atomic bomb project. It's almost the southernmost ski area in the United States. *The* southernmost is Mt. Lemmon, near Tucson, Arizona, sixty miles north of Nogales. (Mt. Lemmon is one of five ski areas in Arizona. The largest, Arizona Snow Bowl, has a two-mile trail and ten-gallon Texans, too.)

The second half of the second century of sport skiing has seen revolutionary changes in ski clothes and equipment. The somber, khaki-clad skiers of the 1920's, their shapeless stuff billowing above soggy leather boots and their wretchedly-conceived wooden runners suitable only for primitive paddling about in the snow, have been replaced by Star Trek characters sheathed in glowing hues of elastic and gossamer, cunningly stretched and insulated. They are shod in shining artifacts capable of esoteric performance. Only the most begrudging would deny the benefits—and only the most sanguine enthuse over the economics—of it all.

The first quantum leap in skis came when the northern countries of Europe started making compound skis—birch soled with hard, heavy hickory—thus gaining a reduction in weight without sacrificing longevity. But lamination could accomplish more. Skis were constructed in multiple layers, not all of them running the full length of the ski. Desirable characteristics could be built in; a certain stiffness here, suppleness there, strength here, weight-saving there. The first superskis emerged from Austria—Kneissl and Kaestle— just in time to send the Austrian *Wunder* team (Toni Sailer *et al.*) on its merry career through the flags.

Wooden Kneissls and Kaestles cost as much as $80 a pair, required the maintenance of a racing Porsche, and even then would all too frequently "explode" into constituent laminations upon striking some half-buried object. The most artful of the wooden skis were the most mortal. Wooden skis made to last forever were not, alas, very good to ski on.

The solution to this miserable problem was propounded by a stork-legged, six-foot five-inch Baltimore aircraft engineer named Howard Head, a determined but not sinuously graceful skier. Head spent five years of evenings in his cellar trying to devise a satisfactory ski made of the classic aircraft material, aluminum. After hitting upon the idea of using aluminum as the stress-bearing skin and wood as a core, Head managed to produce the everlastingly famous Model T of modern skiing, the Head Standard. This ski and its successors enabled Head to retire with some millions of dollars. The ensuing technological fallout hasn't stopped yet.

What was so good about metal? The ski would not warp, break, or shatter except under extreme circumstances, such as being run over by a snow tractor. Even then, it could be bent back into shape. But reliability was less important than the skiability of the Standard. The characteristics of metal can be varied more than those of laminated wood within the length of a ski. The Standard had a soft tip, much softer than could be countenanced on a wooden ski, and a rugged middle section to take the thrust of the skier's weight.

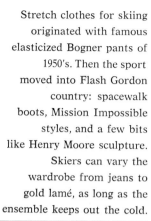

Stretch clothes for skiing originated with famous elasticized Bogner pants of 1950's. Then the sport moved into Flash Gordon country: spacewalk boots, Mission Impossible styles, and a few bits like Henry Moore sculpture. Skiers can vary the wardrobe from jeans to gold lamé, as long as the ensemble keeps out the cold.

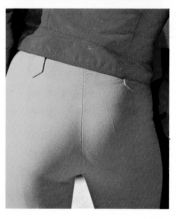

At the same time, it was thin, and sliced deep snow beautifully. The Standard cushioned moguls and turned smoothly when set on edge. The Standard, known as the Cheater, was the beloved of all maidens, beginners, and mogul bashers. But it passed away in the 1970's, when metal for a time was unable to hold its own against fiberglass.

The analogy with the Model T unfolded. Head showed that it was easier to train men to do piecework on manufactured materials with standard properties than to teach them to craft wood with all its intrinsic variations. The ski field became the province of the industrialist, not the guilds. The adaptation of fiberglass to the needs of skiers accelerated the process wildly. There now are hundreds of ski makers, dozens of whom make excellent skis. Head got along with one or two models for decades; manufacturers now produce as many models as their imaginations permit and the market will bear. Each season skis are introduced at top price and at the top of the line, and then arbitrarily drop in price and position a year or two later to make room for a glamorous new top model.

Advertising has been all too persuasive. Metal was virtually wiped out by a heavily cultivated boom in fiberglass. The somewhat different properties of fiberglass that give a smoother ride and extra cushioning do not, however, replace entirely the best qualities of the metal ski, which finally is coming back. Fiberglass skis generally go sluggish after two or three years of hard use. Metal lasts two or three times that before fatiguing.

After 1960, seesaw competition produced skis whose performance exceeded anything that was possible in the 1950's. At the same time, the ski prices tripled. Many average skiers paid $200 a pair for a potential performance that far exceeded their skill. Fancy skis in such cases are less suited to needs than to ego. The fact is that your average first- and second-year skier could have been reasonably accommodated with a pair of $40 Elans, wood skis still being made in Europe in the 1970's. The good life was sold dear.

The evolution of the ski boot is a different story. The average ski boot that sold for $45 in the 1970's is more of a bargain for the average skier than the $45 boot sold in the 1950's. The improvement lies in the change-over from leather and handcraft to artificial materials and machine tending. Leather boots stretched, had a limited life, required costly handcraft labor. Properly made boots of artificial materials do not. Even if prices for the best boots have doubled, they can be a lifetime investment.

Contemporary boots are shaped for specific kinds of skiing. High backs enable hot dogs to do sit-back turns, and high uppers place the strain of setting a proper edge onto the shins and knees (because the ankles move very little in a stiff boot)—an altogether drastic change in technique. In stiff boots, the movement of the knees back and forth over the skis replaced the roll of the ankles for proper edging, a change that called for greater concentration but put the strain where it was better able to be borne over the course of the day, something well appreciated by middle-aged skiers.

In an analogy to the metal tennis racket, which rehabilitated many an aging, aching elbow, the stiff boot has rendered the ankle tendons of the middle-aged skier inviolate. Young skiers made use of the new boots to extend the limits of possible attacks. The kind of inspired bashing that goes on in the mogul fields today would be impossible in a leather boot of the 1950's. So would the kind of descents made by Sylvain Saudan, who depends on the high, stiff back of his boots to make his "turns on the tails."

There was a minor flaw. The doctors at the medical centers in Aspen, Vail, and Sun Valley, where statistics on breaks and traumas are assiduously compiled, noted an epidemic of hairline fractures of the fibula, the small bone on the outside of the shin. The villain was the high boot, of course, which transferred all that pressure from the ankles to the leg bone.

Quest for stretch clothes
started with racers
who wanted tight fit to
cut wind resistance.
(Old-time racers used to
tape their baggy pants.)
A development of
this is the one-piece
racing stretch suit (r).

Skiing is big business.
The industry takes in
$1.5 billion a year,
a good portion from
clothes. Demonstrating
ski fashions is a
source of income over and
above skiing on the
patrol or teaching.
Opposite: Vail's big
name, Roger Staub, former
world champion, does his
bit—and girls do theirs.

The hairline is mostly the bugaboo of skiers who have overbought their boots, got them higher and stiffer than needed for their kind of skiing and for their vitality and technique. The stronger and younger skier can, willy-nilly, survive the attack on the fibula; the cure is usually simply to remain off skis for several weeks. The older skier can rely on cunning execution to reduce pressure on the fibula. The natural hairline victim is the one who has neither cunning nor youth.

When it comes to clothing, skiers have resisted the impossible and opted for the sensible, quite the opposite of their attitude toward skis. The overriding function of ski clothes is to keep the skier warm. Weakness in the main function is readily detected. This gives fashion a hard row to hoe in selling skiwear. Suits of light material appropriate for the greenhouse tan and for lounging by the fireplace did not go far with skiers, although they appeared regularly in the magazines. Most skiers' enthusiasm is reserved for un-fashion innovations like the quilted parka and the warm-up pant.

The quilted parka was the inspiration of mountaineering types who wanted to take cozy eider down feathers with them into cold high altitudes. They compensated for the annoying propensity of down to ball and cluster by designing garments that segregated the feathers in small pockets, like grandmother's quilt.

Gerry in Seattle was the first to come out with down-quilted skiers' jackets. Their superior warmth was soon so evident (particularly in the East) that the old poplin parka backed by two or three heavy sweaters—the classic defense of the 1930's and 40's against frosty ribs—was as passé as the baggy khaki and puttees of the 1920's. Synthetic insulating fibers have somewhat replaced down as a filler, but to get the utmost in warmth for the minimum in weight, skiers still are obliged to the eider duck.

The warm-up pant, which also often is quilted, has a racing origin (like the stretch pant). In the

The equipment world:
In racing, the way the ski
is cared for (opposite) is most
serious. So is what your
competitor is wearing. And
ill-fitting boots are disaster.
Ski shops that pay close
attention to such things as the
picking of a boot will thrive.

The best skiing equipment evolved from the proving ground of racing. Present-day gear is fancy and freewheeling, but very sophisticated in function and quite subtle in response. Price of perfection is high, but most skiers are more than willing to pay for it. Head, K-2 (above), two U.S. makers, produce top quality.

retire to the rest room, strip, find a locker for the bulky underwear and emerge cooler, but having missed at least one ride down the mountain for the day.

The warm-up pant, on the other hand, could be quickly unzipped while standing in the liftline and tucked around the waist or into a fanny pack. For intermediate stages of cooling it could be zipped up halfway on each leg, a picturesque and acceptable dress, like a cowboy's chaps.

The warm-up pant spelled the downgrading of the stretch pant; what one wears under a warm-up pant is less important. A pair of corduroy street pants or jeans will do. And does. That means a considerable saving. The heyday of sleekly modeled stretch pants meant investing a minimum of $40, a maximum of $70. Your warm-up could be bought for $10 to $15—or $20, if fancy. The stretch pant did not die, but is limited mainly to the West. The cost, the considerable problem of keeping it stretched by an elastic stirrup under the foot, its tendency to bag at the knees—all have passed unmourned by one-time wearers of stretchies.

Not that the stretch pant did not have its historical functions. A principal one, aside from racing, where it reduced wind resistance, was to bring several million people into the sport—primarily, it would seem in retrospect, to legitimize wearing such a stunning item. No commentator of current life styles after 1945 could write about skiing without considerable mention of the stretch pant and its presumably aphrodisiac effects on the ski populace.

The original stretch pant was a Bogner, and the name became synonymous with the product. A Bogner was a stretchie. The Bogner family started out in Austria as pedestrian suppliers of work clothes to Norwegian coal miners, among others. The tough cloth that kept miners from having coal-studded kneecaps turned out to be just the thing for skiing, speeds having gotten high enough and the trails hard enough to cause rapid deterioration of pant material in any contact with the snow that lasted more than a tenth of a second.

1960's, racers who needed to keep leg muscles warm while waiting for their number to come up at the starting gate began to wear a quilted pant over the racing stretch pant. In order to come off quickly at the start of the race, without having to undo the meticulously buckled-up boots, warm-up pants had full-length zippers on each side of the pant, from cuff to belt. This feature made it invaluable for ordinary recreational skiers as well. The pre-1960's method for keeping the legs warm was quilted or double-layer underwear beneath the stretch pant. Unfortunately, as the day warmed, the only way to reduce heat under the stretch pant (which could be considerable) was to

The paraphernalia that
constitutes the periphery of
ski fashion is endless:
goggles, scarves, suntan creams,
lotions, socks—all those
things that make for the compleat
skier. Here is a selection
piled on the counter
of Gorsuch, Ltd., in Vail.

From there, once the stretch fabric was invented, the path to the classic Bogner was clear. The degeneration of the genre into hostess pants may have had something to do with the alacrity with which many serious skiers abandoned the stretchie in the 1970's.

If history is a spiral sort of progress, the 1970's saw a re-entry loop into the oldest kind of ski clothes, the touring style. The reappearance of the long wool knee sock, the natty knicker, and the pattern sweater—backed up by quilted equipment if necessary—proves something. *Plus ça change, plus c'est la même chose,* as the French say.

Hats: The ski hat, like the sport, came in two models, one from the Scandinavian hills, the other from the heights of the Alps. The Scandinavian knitted hat, in various forms, is still very much alive for the reason that one size fits many heads, and thus it is cheaply made and easily pulled over the ears for warmth without reducing hearing. The Austrians, on the other hand, favored what became known here as the Sun Valley hat, a visored king-size golf cap with let-down ear flaps. It was worn by Count Felix Scaffgotsch, the discoverer of Sun Valley. Consequently it had the loyalty of other Sun Valley skiers, including Averell Harriman, the man whose railroad underwrote the Sun Valley venture. Sadly, the aesthetic was flawed. The hat transformed the wearer into a dumbfounded radio operator listening to an SOS. Aside from making people's heads look narrow, Sun Valley hats successfully prevented them from hearing what was said, and they tended to fly off at speed higher than ten miles an hour. Accordingly, Sun Valley hats are no longer with us. Their best days came during World War II with the Tenth Mountain in Italy, where they were darn good for keeping down the noise of the guns.

There is, of course, the aberrant "bunny hat," a fuzzy, usually pink concoction made of—ugh—angora, which usually arrives at the slope in a bus. A variation of this gaucherie is the purloined World War I aviator's helmet which was popular with the drag-racing set. The only skier I knew who wittingly wore one was Dudley Doust, a compatriot of mine at *Sports Illustrated.* But then Dudley was the only skier I knew who never—actually—bent his knees, either. And his remaining garb was individual as well. One windy winter afternoon in the 1950's, Dudley, whose vestments then included a pair of telephone lineman's boots he'd fitted into bear-trap bindings, workpants taped around the ankles, plus a surplus knee-length Army parka with a hood lined in rabbit fur, preceded me across the parking lot at Killington. He leaned against the wind with all his ties and laces whipping in his lee, for all the world like a tattered square-rigger washing through the sea five years out. On the other side of the lot, incredulous, stood Pres Smith, who had lately founded Killington. When Dudley finally made it to Pres's side, Pres seized him by both shoulders, looked into Dudley's eyes, and said, huskily, "Take me to your leader."

Occasionally, I teach beginners to ski. Once, coincidentally, I had a group—on skis for the first time—that was very diverse: a successful New York bandleader, his girl, a high-school dropout, and a native Samoan newly arrived in the United States who had never seen snow. The results were approximately the same. All were uniformly ecstatic at being allowed to turn, fall, arise, and live to turn again in the midst of the large crowd of skiers. Then, having been able, all of them, to ski from the top to the bottom of Bromley on their second day on three-foot GLM skis, they repaired to the Pabst Parlor at Bromley with their instructor.

Their wide-ranging backgrounds were as nothing compared to the world into which they'd been thrown. The good life for them began that afternoon in the Pabst Parlor. Without the preceding skiing, the after-skiing would have been just another drink in another bar. It wasn't. It was a jubilation. They were all brimming with a ski "high." Their eyes laughed, their faces were alight, and they talked easily and happily. Some of that stays with all skiers, and it is what makes the good life good.

Skiing, too, observes the seasons. In autumn, light snow dusts the gold-and-red fire of fallen leaves in New England and salts the cool, blue-green glacial ice of the Alpine massif. In the fullness of winter the snow creaks, the fury of the Sierra blizzard buries the Donner Pass once again, the peaks of the Kitzbühler Alps are sharks' teeth raking a solid blue sky. In March the sun is higher, and there is coarse soft snow and the scent of redwoods in Squaw Valley. In spring the stream starts up under the skier's track at Tuckerman's. We are at the divide, about to pass into the season of no skiing.

Springtime is a mixed joy. The impending absence of skiing is no easy matter. Yet spring is also a time of relaxation. The level of the sport each skier has reached must suffice. In the comfort of warm days and clear skies the lassitude that hibernates during the sharp, steely winds of winter reappears.

Spring skiing can be prolonged by taking to altitudes beyond those safely available in the winter. Along the Haute Route, in the high Cariboo, on the glaciers of Mt. Baker, or the rolling fells of Kitzsteinhorn one can postpone the pain of leave-taking. But the delay has finite limits. A week or two, perhaps three or four. Then it's over.

It's over—unless herculean efforts are made. But a chase around the world for an endless winter has its own hazards. The annual rhythm of skiing and not-skiing constitutes a part of skiing's delight. Much may be lost in surfeit. The young skier may be able to force three years' worth of progress into two by alternating antipodal-winter and northern-winter skiing. But progress in technique generally proceeds just as quickly in the natural swings of the season. The equation, progress equals time on the snow, has not been proved.

But there is nevertheless pleasure in extending the transitional skiing of spring in its special places. A most famous spring locale in the American East is Tuckerman's Ravine, a glacial cirque above Pinkham Notch on the eastern slope of Mt. Washington. The Snowfields, that part of Mt. Washington immediately above the Ravine, are included, too. Skiing here may last well into June. Mostly the snow lies above 5,000 feet, double the altitude that supports New England skiing during its winter season.

The skiing in Tuckerman's is completely apart from all other eastern skiing. In the first place, it is the only place where otherwise reluctant eastern alpine skiers willingly walk uphill, on skis and off. Skiers have been walking up the Fire Trail from Pinkham Notch since the 1930's. The Sherbourne, the below-timberline descending trail, the second half of the famous Inferno course, was one of the first trails cut in the East and one of the few old-timers not paired with a lift by the end of the 1940's.

The most dramatic running of the famous Mt. Washington Inferno race—so difficult to hold without lifts that it has been run full-length only twice in history—was in 1939, when a very young Toni Matt, from Austria, won it. Matt had come over to teach at North Conway and was racing so well that he cut 10 and 15 seconds off the best previous times.

On this occasion the course was from the peak of Mt. Washington down the steepest section of the Ravine, the Headwall, where snow blowing over the edge forms a half-dome. The transition is like going over the rounded tiles at the edge of a swimming pool that is a thousand feet deep. What made the 1939 race famous was that Matt simply schussed the whole thousand-foot Headwall—took it straight. No one who raced in those days, outside of Matt, had even thought of the possibility.

Matt came off the bottom of the Headwall at about 85 miles per hour, rocketed across the floor, down the Little Headwall, onto the Sherbourne, and down to Pinkham Notch, 60 full seconds ahead of the runner-up, Dick Durrance. Matt was so fatigued by the incredible six-minute run that he almost didn't make it. Just before the last turn on the Sherbourne, he caught an edge and headed for a tree. He heaved

himself back on the trail with a grunt heard all the way to the finish line.

The difficulty of the descent and the fact that the Ravine is a two-hour walk up, and that it's steep as hell and occasionally dangerous, even in spring, make the legend of Tuckerman's what it is. The Ravine still draws its crowd of spring skiers, even though today the famous "Howard Johnson's" shelter at the bottom has been torn down and the number of tents restricted. Carrying your tent up and skiing the Headwall for a weekend has always been a rite of spring, and still is.

The Ravine avalanches all winter. The walls are 45 to 60 degrees steep (the latter figure is the highest that will hold snow at all). Wet spring snow settles nicely and does not avalanche. Then the only problem is ice. The ice forms on the Ravine wall during spring and comes off in big hunks. A thirty- or forty-pound piece of ice hurtling down the wall can kill. Some chunks are bigger than that. During the day a cry of "Ice!" will occasionally be heard from the skiers running lazily at the bottom of the enormous white reflector oven formed by the cirque. A big piece will come bounding down like a crazed jackrabbit. The thing to do is to observe which way it goes and —not too soon—run the other way. (A few years ago a doctor panicked and ran too early. The ice changed course and hit him squarely in the back. He died before they got him out of the Ravine.)

The Headwall is one run I have never skied. I almost skied it. My friend, Bill Hazen, and I climbed the Fire Trail one day in the 1940's, with blood in our eye. We were going to do it. Ski the Wall. And so we headed for the old Harvard Hut, built many years before by the Harvard Outing Club and then still standing. A free night's stay. It was a bitter cold dusk when we arrived. It was colder inside the hut than out, and that is saying a lot. I tried but couldn't get a fire started in the old Franklin stove. The wood was too cold. Spotting a can of kerosene, I sloshed some over the wood. A flash of flame

shot from the stove, which I had thought completely dead, and jumped to the can, which ignited. I threw it away from me into a corner and kerosene splattered over the corner walls, which promptly caught fire. Bill and I rushed out for armfuls of snow to throw against the sizzling walls. By the time we had the fire out, cleaned the mess, and cooked dinner it was eleven P.M. We were exhausted. We got up late and started climbing—and then the whole mountain fogged in. I'll run it someday.

A feature of the ridge of the Wasatch range outside Great Salt Lake is a huge cirque below the peak of Timpanogos. Here the snow stays dry until the end of May. Unless you have the time to climb it, you board a helicopter at Provo and fly to it. There it is, the last powder of the winter, all fifty acres of it.

The day I went, getting there was half the excitement. A wild wind was blowing up the Salt Lake side of Timpanogos. It arched over and came slamming down into the bowl in drafty gusts, making it unsafe to land inside. The only place the helicopter pilot could set us down was on the very rim of the wall—"inside the curl," as he put it—a dead-air space. The first attempt was a failure. The copter's nose stuck into the stream of wind coming up the wall and the updraft, like an invisible elevator cable, lifted the copter straight up.

One more try. Same thing. Third try, the copter yo-yoed slightly, six feet over the snow, hovered long enough for us to get out and throw our skis down on the snow. We hunched to keep the prop blast from knocking us down the mountain. John Zimmerman, the cameraman on hand to record the story, almost bought it. He slid over the rim while using both hands to protect his camera and only kept from sliding a long way by slamming both elbows into the snow, like ice axes.

But, ah, the powder! The day was a blue vault overhead and the bowl skied like silk. We made tracks reverently, for we knew these were our last for a while and then, after two miles of running, finally, reluctantly, we let ourselves slip over the far side of the cirque, down into warmer air layers

Opening pages: State of Washington's Mt. Baker has skiable snow through most of summer, and a lounging skier can soak up the sun while extending his season, getting the same tan as his friends on beaches.

The end of the ski season means a delightful snow known as corn. It's forgiving, middle-aged snow, happy to be of use to skiers, whether found at Telluride (above & opposite), Mt. Washington, New Hampshire (above r), or Alyeska, Alaska (r). But it signals that the time of not-skiing is at hand. So these are scenes of parting.

and the actuality of spring that was flowing up to meet us, and down into Sundance, the resort at the very bottom of Timpanogos, six miles from the high, heaven-reaching walls we had lately known.

The most popular spring place in the Rockies is Arapahoe Basin, which has the highest base of any resort in the world: 10,800 feet. The vertical is not exceptional—2,500—but there is a steep run, Palivacinni, which is fabulous skiing in the spring. It's a chute with about the same drop—38 degrees—as the Headwall. Palivacinni is prime avalanche territory and a test of reflexes.

Arapahoe is the rendezvous place for those not yet ready to give up. It can be cold far into May, sometimes all the way to June on the upper lift. Here come the instructors, free of their classes at last, and the racers free of the flags. The sun is out almost every day and the diehard Denver skiers, only a couple of hours away, can commute without having to spend a nickel on lodging. There is only dust to worry about. The desert sirocco can ruin aesthetics. At Arapahoe I directed a film produced by Roger Brown called *Five Days to Ski;* we took ten nonskiers from Denver up there in early April, and Karl Pfeiffer taught them all how to ski parallel in five days. It's there on film. What's also on the film is red dust. A desert storm dropped a rusty sheen over all and we filmed the proceedings on red snow.

Big Mountain, in Whitefish, Montana, is another spot that hits its stride in spring. Big Mountain is 5,000 at the base and 2,200 more vertical feet to the top, way up there next to the Canadian border, a lonely outpost in Glacier National Park. Cool spring temperatures combine with a northern exposure, so that Big Mountain snow cover is preserved until May 15, or later. And it has a magnificent run, the Face. A hundred feet from the lift it breaks downward, a 40-degree slope that leaves you hanging over two beautiful emerald lakes in the green forests below.

Big Mountain is a scene of post-season instructors' rallies, where the biggies get together to conduct seminars and business in general. (Ski-teaching is a business, after all.) At the National Rally at Big Mountain in 1956, the instructors first formed their national organization—the Professional Ski Teachers of America. They adopted the now-defunct American System. It was a big day. When it came time to demonstrate wedel as part of the System, the only skiers who could do it consistently were European instructors. It was a little embarrassing. This crazy scene, with the best American instructors trying to wedel and falling all over themselves, is part of what I think of as spring.

The Sierra spring focuses on Mammoth, in Southern California. Skiers shying away from spring ascend Mammoth's high saddle and look down at the encroaching green coming on like a Martian virus. I climbed the saddle one spring before the big gondola went up there. The procedure was: First, take a snow cat up to the ravine, throw your skis and poles over the side onto the floor of the ravine, climb down after them, and then climb up the main saddle, a good three-hour jaunt. On top we took a good hour of sun, peeled to the waist, drank Liebfraumilch from bottles and, fortified for the ordeal, skied on down toward the green crawling up at us.

One does not have to go to Tuckerman's, Arapahoe, Whitefish, or Mammoth—big-deal places—to say farewell in an appropriate way. It's possible right near home. One year when I was working on the *Laconia Citizen* in New Hampshire, we local skiers had a fine last-day rite at Belknap (now called Gunstock), a last nip up the old rope tow, one more time down Tiger. The Tiger rope was a special sort of rope. Halfway up, the first rope looped up over a return pulley and you had to reach forward and grasp a second rope, which descended from its pulley an arm's length away. Hard enough to do sober. Four of us out of eight made it to the top. Tiger was about gone. The only continuous piece of snow was the packed ski track under the rope. But the four of us skied down, gelandespringing from patch to patch, like four Elizas escaping

The zigzag of climbing skiers leaves a geometrical track to fade with the advancing season. This group is moving through snowfields above Chamonix, looking down on the clouds, and missing winter's crowd not at all.

the bloodhounds. We lost the last of our base wax (that's what it was in those days) and a not inconsiderable amount of wood off the bottom of our skis going over the grass and rocks.

At all resorts in spring, aside from the lunacy of the slush races, there's always an Easter Parade. A prize goes to the most glorious costume in the group. One year, it is said, unofficial Honorable Mention at Mt. Snow went to a small but buxom lass who, in the midst of clown costumes and kids in bunny suits, pranced around the judging ring in skis, boots, and nothing else—besides a natural pulchritude. Not bad for a family area.

The only lifts that really get above treeline in the East are at Sugarloaf in Maine. The snow above treeline there looks great all winter, but the skiing is tough except on those rare days when the wind lets up enough for the snow to lie. In spring, however, the snow on top turns to sugar —large, delightful granules. Sugarloaf stays open until May just to make the point that they're the last to close in the East, and skiing the white top is almost enough to ease the pain of another season's ending.

Sugarloaf's white top was what first got Amos Winter interested in it. Amos ran a general store in nearby Kingfield, and when business was slow, he'd get out his homemade, solid-pine skis with the bear-trap bindings. He'd slog up as far as he could, and ski some more on a trail he was cutting from the treeline down. Winter's Way was the first steep trail in Maine. It's still there among the welter of Sugarloaf's newer trails, and Amos is still there, or was last I looked, seventy years strong, still playing tennis in summer and skiing in winter.

Two dozen summer racing camps now operate in the U.S., starting in spring, a phenomenon that derives its success from two sources: the difficulty fledgling racers encounter getting enough training sandwiched between school courses, and the lack of a good, solid, ten-day winter vacation for racers and hackers alike. In summer racing camp, the racer can get ten days of instruction and ten to twenty days of just plain skiing on snow that lies cool on the top of permanent glaciers. The camps are not just for racers. The summer ski instructor will take a stem skier and give him a ten-day course that is the equivalent of a winter's worth of weekends. The stem duckling will come out a parallel swan.

Billy Kidd wrote in *Ski*: "Improvement of ski ability is not a racing camp's only aim. In a day when hard work, discipline, consideration for others and self-control are not stressed as strongly in our society as they once were, summer camps take up the slack. Personally speaking, one of my greatest rewards as a camp instructor was seeing one of the most ill-disciplined kids I'd ever met turn into one of the most enthusiastic, pleasant ski racers we had in camp. It took two summer sessions, but we felt we had produced a youngster who would be a credit to skiing as well as to society."

Another manifestation of spring is "ski-Jeeping." Telluride is the newest of the Colorado ski cities but a long-time capital of spring ski-Jeeping. The mining roads go up into the snow ridges above the town, above the lifts, on and on into the high back-country where the spring snow stays long after the streets of Telluride are dusty. There's bowl after bowl of soft, willing snow, and the red Colorado rock cliffs have startling waterfalls cascading toward the valleys. The break-up of winter above Telluride is a magnificent pageant. Skiing in the soft airs of April is a skier's last warm embrace of his sport.

Way up north in the Rockies, the helicopters whirr and whirl all spring around the Bugaboos, Cariboos, and Monashees. But there is a more spring-like and idyllic way to go into the British Columbia Rockies. Take one of the uphill-bound, Hans Gmoser ski-camping trips. The vertical that took ten minutes in a helicopter may take a day or two on foot, but it's the difference between hiking and driving. The mountains come alive in the spring. From 500 feet up, in a helicopter, or skiing down at 30 miles an hour, you miss most of that. The people who hike on skis see the delicate buds on the spruce and the quicksilver ripple of small streams washing away their winter ice cover. A ski climb has its special rewards: the simply fabulous feeling of just sitting down at the end of the day, not to mention the ambience around a campfire throwing wavering rings of light into the night.

Another redoubtable bastion against springtime lies in the American Northwest, where the snows of Mt. Hood, Mt. Baker, and Whistler get deeper, even as the snow cover shrinks all around. On the Northwest's highest peaks, snow lies twenty feet deep in April. The spring tours on Mt. Hood go to 8,500 feet by snow cat, and then it's a 500-foot vertical on foot, and a 45-minute traverse to the Eliat Glacier country on the mountain's far side. Skiing down 6,000 vertical feet to Cooper's Spur will take your mind off summer. This is real ski mountaineering, turning through the huge juts of striated rock and roping across the steeper and slipperier traverses. In between, the snow is like white velvet, set off by huge seracs and bordered by crevasses as magnificent and chilling as anything in the Alps. In Hood Valley below, the season is heralded

by the delicate shades of apple trees in bloom. It's May.

Near Bend, Mt. Bachelor has a lift that goes over spring snow, and deep drifts that defy the rising thermometer. The last third of the way to the top is a hike, but worth it. The nice thing about spring skiing at Bachelor is that it involves a natural tapering-off process. By noon, the snow gets too wet to ski, so the skiers get up early, ski until lunch, and spend the afternoon playing tennis or going for bike rides— all those things that can get one used to the idea that there is really something else to do. Billy Kidd recalled once when he spent all morning on Mt. Bachelor and all afternoon drifting down the Deschutes River out of Bend in an inner tube.

Mt. Baker in Washington, even farther north, has a vast plateau above timberline that for years has been the province of the skier with an appetite for uphill going. There are miles of milk-smooth skiing here, and the setting sun throws a flame on the barns among the green hills below, where farmers are planting the first crop.

The top of Whistler, outside Vancouver, is another last resort. There's always an Onagin helicopter waiting around for good weather to go whirling into the back country. Whistler is a rugged, rough mountain, beloved of the last of the tough skiers. As traffic thins out toward spring, the snow of the trails is left the way it falls, and the good crud skier can make his mark. Sometimes the advent of spring brings a ferocity to the tough skier's style, as if to drive out the idea that it is all going to be over. I saw Dag Aaby, one of the tough skiers of history, break a binding in the middle of Whistler, inspect it, throw the ski over his shoulder and continue down, bouncing from turn to turn on the remaining ski in mashed-potato snow. He went out of sight in a high gelandy over a drop.

Behind Whistler, the Garibaldi Glacier runs provide lovely skiing boulevards. Skiers can turn without thought of obstacles for well over a couple of miles. This, plus warm weather and hot sun, can bring on spring madness. One skier, in a helicopter party that included me, got so wound up

High on slopes of Mt. Hood, two summer skiers, seduced by sun, plant their skis as back rests and use discarded clothing to pillow their indolence. When in winter would a little sun halt the downhill run?

that he kept turning and turning with such metronomic regularity that he simply couldn't leave off. He went by the rest of us shouting, "I can't stop! I can't stop!" He later claimed 210 consecutive turns before his legs went.

Most skiers are going to say their goodbyes in less exotic circumstances. They will be making the final run on slopes where the melt process is sure and swift. By March 30 in New England the gray rocks and the yellow grass start showing under the base of the trails. The snow still is good if you use the right wax. In spring even the alpine skier becomes a wax expert rather than endure the torture of unwilling skis. Red and Silver are the colors of spring.

In two weeks of steady travel on one of my spring itineraries I ticked off Waterville, Cannon, Attitash, Sugarloaf, Pleasant, Stowe, Mad River, Killington, Ascutney, Mt. Snow. In these places skiers had no thoughts of the high, white, dry Rockies to sustain them. This rock and weed and snow was all they had. They were making the most of it. They didn't even have the grace to be sad about it.

At Mt. Snow I chatted with Walt Schoenknecht, who was holding forth on a rapid-transit system that was to operate on cables among the Green Mountains to gather the skiers to the lifts without the intervention of the auto. Outside the window the skiers ran up and down the rapidly thinning snow. A black fog lowered and rose over the mountain like a candle snuffer. A warm monsoon howled up over the back side. Except where the snow-making machines had layered their spill, grass patches strung the mountain. Even so, sheets of snow saturated with water infested the trails, making slush splatter to both sides. But here were thousands of skiers cutting through as if they were in the finest powder—with glee.

The future is not always what present indicators predict, but it's inconceivable that skiing has anything less than an assured and expanding place in American leisure. The desire to ski is strongly manifested by the sport's clientele even in the difficult conditions of the American Northeast; how much more sanguine the outlook for other places more fortunate in their weather and snow.

Neither snow machines nor teaching methods make the sport the resource that it is. The doing itself is the reward. Other things just make it more possible, and the more possible, the more skiers. The birth rate of new skiers used to hinge on the development of facilities by imposing benefactors—Starr of Stowe, Harriman of Sun Valley, and Walter Paepcke of Aspen—and Container Corporation. (Steve Miller, in his days as master of ceremonies of the show at the Golden Horn in Aspen, had a standard line that went, "And now, I want to introduce Mr. Possible, the man who made all this Paepcke.") But the days of the patron have gone and this is the day of the corporation, manned to a great extent by kids taking up a life in the mountains, kids who would have been the ski bums of the older resorts but are the driving force of the new. Vail and Killington, the biggest in America, are only the outstanding examples.

The business acumen of the new generation is tempered with respect for ecological values. The idea of the best new resorts is to synthesize country life and city life—preserving the beauty and physical challenge of the one, the sophistication and convenience of the other. Something good could come of this. Or it could, at worst, be a stage in the eventual disappearance of the best values of life in mountain country. The outcome is in the hands of the people who have come to the mountains. They may succeed in setting a strong course away from the shoals of overdevelopment.

The millions now on skis will at least effect an increase in the number of dedicated skiers able to celebrate the sport in appropriate ways. It is in the nature of mountains to have a certain resistance. To subdue that to the point where it can no longer challenge skiers is hopefully something far beyond man's capacity and certainly beyond the desire of all who go to the mountains.

This is effectively the end. Here in Colorado the snow has run out and summer's arrival can no longer be delayed. The time for the mountain to restore itself is at hand and the song of the skier fades throughout the land.

BIBLIOGRAPHY

America's Ski Book, Editors of Ski Magazine (Scribner's, New York). An encyclopedic approach to most of the subjects associated with the sport, concluding with a table of resorts.

The Book of European Skiing, Malcolm N. H. Milne and Mark Heller, eds. (Holt, Rinehart and Winston, New York). A good look at European techniques, with some general comments on skiing in Europe. The section on Scandinavia is particularly good.

Eastern Ski Atlas (National Survey, Chester, Vermont). Six pages of regional ski maps plus seventy pages giving tabular summaries of 300 ski areas in the eastern U.S., including Ontario and Quebec. Advertisements of the areas and lodges are included.

A Guide to Western Skiing, Curtis Casewit (Chronicle Books, San Francisco). Reliable evaluations of twenty-three top resorts in the West, including Banff and Whistler, with getting-there information as well.

How The Racers Ski, Warren Witherell (W. W. Norton, New York). The first good book by an American on racing—from bindings to back lean.

The New York Times Guide to Ski Areas, USA, Michael Strauss (Quadrangle Books, New York). Concisely tabulated facts (prices, phone numbers, verticals, lifts) with short comments on four-hundred-odd top U.S. resorts.

Nordic Touring and Cross Country Skiing, M. Michael Brady (Arthur Vanous Co., Hackensack, New Jersey). The classic racing styles illustrated, with good equipment information.

The Pleasures of Cross Country Skiing, Morten Lund (Outerbridge and Lazard, New York; Avon, New York). Illustrated with picture sequences, this teaches correct touring stride and techniques for climbing and downhill on cross-country skis; gives advice, too, on winter camping, cooking out, and ski mountaineering.

Ski Europe, Egon Ronay (British Automobile Association, London). The most complete listing of European resorts, including those in Sweden, Spain, and Scotland. Lift lengths, elevations, and prices, but little useful evaluation. It comes with a fold-out map of European resort locations.

Ski GLM, Morten Lund (Dial, New York). The major methods of teaching on short skis, as they have developed in the U.S., including the Taylor System, Headway, and American Teaching Method.

Ski Guide to Europe, Abby Rand (Award House and Crown, New York). The best of the European guides, packed full of practical consumer advice on accommodations and après-ski for the forty major European ski locales.

Ski Magazine's Encyclopedia of Skiing (Harper & Row, New York). An up-dated version of *America's Ski Book,* more comprehensive in its treatment of ski technique. Lavishly illustrated, with a large, well-written travel section.

Ski New Horizons, Roland Palmedo (Simon & Schuster, New York). Brief descriptions and travel information for some of the world's excellent but little-known ski resorts.

Ski North America, Abby Rand (Lippincott, Philadelphia). Accommodation and price information for the top twenty-eight American resorts, and best ways to get there. Shrewd evaluations of the hotels, inns, and après-ski.

The Ski Runs of Austria and **The Ski Runs of Switzerland,** James Riddell (Michael Joseph, London). A thorough description of the important lift runs of these two countries, and line maps of the largest resorts. No accommodation or price information.

Skier's Bible, Morten Lund (Doubleday, New York). The only book that compares the major teaching methods from the point of view of the skier: short ski, direct parallel, the classic Austrian, and the American Teaching Method. Included is a primer on ski travel and equipment.

Skier's Paradise, Morten Lund and Bob Laurie (Putnam's, New York). The hundred best ski trails in North America and how to ski them, with a summary of the resorts themselves.

Skiing Simplified, Douglas Pfeiffer (Grosset & Dunlap, New York). A good treatise on body positions, pole work, and methods of skiing particular terrain; excellent drawings accompany the text.

Skiing Western America, Charles C. Miller (One Hundred One Productions, San Francisco). A personal account of the lodgings, skiing, and après-ski at forty-eight of the world's biggest areas, with quick-reference information of ski schools, equipment rental, lift and lodge rates.

Wilderness Skiing, Lito Tejada-Flores and Allen Steck (Sierra Club, San Francisco). A handy tote-book for the backpacking skier; gets into climbing technique as well.

BK—**Bob Krueger**
B&IS—**Bob and Ira Spring**
BS—**Barry Stott**
DM—**Del Mulkey**
FL—**Fred Lindholm**
FM—**Fletcher Manley**

HC—**Hanson Carroll**
KM—**Kim Massie**
NC—**Norm Clasen**
PM—**Peter Miller**
PR—**Paul Ryan**
PW—**Peter Wingle**

Jacket: **Norm Clasen**
(Credits read from left to right and from top to bottom.)

Chapter 1

10-11: PM. 12-13: PW. 14-15: Fred Dayton (two); FL; KM. 16: DM. 17: DM. 18: Steve Marks; KM. 19: PM. 20: FM. 21: PM. 22-23: NC. 24: DM. 25: PW. 26-27: PM; Takeo Fukishima; KM. 28: PW. 29: Rupert Leser.

Chapter 2

30-31: PM. 34: Dick Durrance; DM; Morten Lund. 35: FL. 36: PW. 38-39: FL. 41: B&IS. 42-43: B&IS. 43: DM; B&IS; DM. 44: B&IS. 46: DM (both). 47: DM. 49: PM. 50-51: PM (all). 52: PW.

Chapter 3

54-55: Morten Lund. 58: PM. 59: PR; PM; NC. 61: J. Naegeli. 62: PR. 63: Ellie Waterston; PM; PR; DM. 64: HC. 66: Morten Lund; PM (three); Dick Durrance. 67: PM. 69: Neil M. Wright; Joern Gerdts; Sue Teipel. 70: Sun Valley News Bureau. 71: PM; BS; Morten Lund; Aspen Ski Corporation.

Chapter 4

74-75: NC. 78: BS; BK; FL. 79: PR. 80: Bill Herbeck. 81: Bruce C. Barthel. 82: BS; BS (center strip); BK (right strip). 83: DM; NC; KM; FL. 86-87: FL. 87: DM; DM; BS. 89: Scott Nelson. 90: BS. 91: BS; BK. 93: BS; Sue Teipel; PM; DM; DM. 94: HC; PM; FM; FM; DM.

Chapter 5

98-99: R. Löbl. 102: PM. 103: PM; HC; PM. 105: R. Löbl. 107: PM; Prov-ince of Salzburg, Austria; Andreas Pedrett. 110: Morten Lund. 111: PM; DM; PM. 112: Photopress. 114: DM; Dick Durrance; PM; PM. 115: PM (all). 117: DM. 118: Scottish Tourist Board; Scottish Council of Physical Education; Scottish Tourist Board. 123: Marvin Newman; KM; Marvin Newman; Marvin Newman.

Chapter 6

126-127: NC. 130-131: PM. 134-135: PM (three); DM. 137: DM. 138-139: DM; BS; PM; KM; BS. 140: BK. 142-143: Bob Chamberlain; NC. 145: BK. 146-147: Sun Valley News Bureau; NC; FL; Aspen Ski Corporation. 150-151: FL. 153: FL. 154-155: NC; FL; NC; FL; PM. 157: Hap Chandler. 158: Joern Gerdts; Takeo Fukishima; FM. 159: DM.

Chapter 7

162-163: PW. 166-167: DM; Peter Schoeck; Steen Svensson; Morton Beebe. 169: Trade en France. 170: National Tourist Organization of Greece. 171: Peter Schoeck. 172: Dick Barrymore; Moroccan Tourist Office. 173: FM. 175: Australian Tourist Commission; Australian News & Information Bureau. 176: Donald Dangely. 177: Rolf Ericson. 178: DM. 179: B&IS.

Chapter 8

182-183: NC. 186: FL. 187: PM; PM; NC; NC; PM. 188: PM; BS; Elaine Mayes; NC. 190: PM; DM; PM; Sun Valley News Bureau. 191: PM (three); DM. 193: PM; NC; DM; BS; BK; NC; NC. 194-195: PM (all). 196: Brod Briggs. 198: Steve Marks. 199: NC; NC; DM; PM. 201: Rupert Leser. 202: HC; Rupert Leser. 203: HC. 204: Rupert Leser.

Chapter 9

206-207: FL. 209: BS. 210: PM. 211: FL; PM; KM; PR. 212: PM. 214: PM; Joern Gerdts. 214-215: PM. 215: BS; PM. 216: PM. 217: Sue Teipel; KM. 218: PM (three); FL. 220: Ron Harris. 222: Ron Harris. 223: Ron Harris; PM; Hal Davis; Ron Harris; PR; PM. 225: BK. 226: FL. 227: BS; BK; PM. 228: Bruce C. Barthel. 229: O. Gangl; NC. 230: BS. 231: FL; Bruce C. Barthel; George Schwartz; BS. 232: BS.

Chapter 10

234-235: DM. 238: DM; Morten Lund; Joern Gerdts. 239: DM. 241: DM. 243: DM. 245: DM.

INDEX